KT-142-160

Hinch Yourself Happy

Hinch Yourself Happy

All the Best Cleaning Tips to
Shine Your Sink and Soothe Your Soul

MRS HINCH

MICHAEL JOSEPH
an imprint of
PENGUIN BOOKS

MICHAEL JOSEPH

UK | USA | Canada | Ireland | Australia
India | New Zealand | South Africa

Michael Joseph is part of the Penguin Random House group of companies
whose addresses can be found at global.penguinrandomhouse.com

First published 2019
008

Copyright © Mrs Hinch, 2019

The moral right of the author has been asserted

Set in 13.5/16pt Garamond MT Std
Typeset by Jouve (UK), Milton Keynes
Printed and bound in Great Britain by Clays Ltd, Elcograf S.p.A.

A CIP catalogue record for this book is available from the British Library

HARDBACK ISBN: 978-0-241-39975-0

www.greenpenguin.co.uk

Penguin Random House is committed to a
sustainable future for our business, our readers
and our planet. This book is made from Forest
Stewardship Council® certified paper.

Publisher's Note: The information in this book has been compiled by way of general guidance only. Nothing in this book is intended as an express or implied warranty of the suitability or fitness of any product or service. The reader wishing to use a product or service discussed in this book should first consult a specialist or professional to ensure suitability and fitness for the reader's particular lifestyle and environmental needs if necessary. Neither the author nor the publisher shall be liable or responsible for any loss or damage allegedly arising from any information or suggestion in this book.

Product Safety: Use cleaning products safely and always follow the following guidelines:
Always read the label and product information before use.
Wear gloves when using cleaning products to protect your hands and wash hands after use.
Carry out a patch test on inconspicuous areas before use of products.
Take care when using any cleaning products around your pets. Do not let cleaning products come into contact with pets and ensure that the cleaned area is dry before allowing pets to come into contact with it.

To My Husband Jamie, My Beautiful Boy Henry Hinch,
My Family, My Friends and My Hinchers

All the Best
Love Soph xx

Contents

PART THREE

A Bit About Me

PART FOUR

Grab Your Minkeh,
We're Going On A Cleaning Adventure

WELCOME, MY WONDERFUL HINCHERS!

This book is for each and every one of you because you guys really are the absolute best. You have genuinely changed my life.

As you have all heard me say many times before, I am not a professional cleaner. I've never claimed to be. But I hope I can help to make the whole process fun for people. I think cleaning (aka hinching) really has the potential to bring people together. Just hear me out on this one . . . you've got all your celebrities and your supermodels, and even those people you just aspire to be like, but remember this, Hinchers, we're all the same when we're wearing a pair of rubber Gregory Gloves and cleaning our toilets. I'm just saying!

Now some may think it strange, but I have such a laugh when I clean, organise or just hinch in general, and I would love everyone to come along with me for the ride. I just do whatever works for me and I try to make it as easy and as enjoyable as possible. I love life and I love to smile . . . you can never smile too much now, can you!

I get asked all sorts of questions about housework, removing stains, limescale, being organised, etc, but believe it or not, especially more recently, I get asked so many more questions about my life in general, so fingers crossed I'll answer them all for you in this book. Hopefully you'll be able to take a lot away from it and pick up tips, just like I have, that will stay with you forever.

If I talked about cleaning but didn't tell you about the positive impact it's had on my life and why I started hinching in the first place, it would feel odd. Cleaning has been my saviour in a lot of ways. I've always been very open about the fact that I am a worrier. I live with anxiety, nerves and panic attacks, but grabbing one of my favourite cloths and getting busy has been the thing that I've found helps to calm my mind more than anything else.

I think it's so important to be upfront and honest about my worrying and panic attacks, and that's why I also wanted to give you an insight into both my past and my present, and explain exactly why my Instagram account means so much to me.

So grab yourself a cuppa and get yourself cosy in your favourite comfy spot in your home, with your favourite throw, and read on, my Hinchers.

All the best,
Mrs Hinch x

PART ONE

Home Is Where My Heart Is

CHAPTER ONE

MY HOME
IS MY
SANCTUARY

My home means everything to me. It means safety and cosiness and happiness. All of my achievements are here and it's mine and Mr Hinch's and Henry's home, and that means the world.

No one knows what really happens behind closed doors. No matter how well we know people, we never truly get to see what happens when they come in, kick off their shoes and hide away. All of your secrets are in the place where you live. You probably have your best and your worst times there, and it's your private treasure chest that only you have a key to.

Anyone can live in a house, flat, apartment or caravan, but making that place a home is the best feeling ever. Now, it goes without saying that what truly makes somewhere homely is the memories that you and your loved ones share there. That obviously is one of the most important things. But from an aesthetic point of view, you can make somewhere your home by putting things you love in it. You decorate it how you like and you keep it clean. You douse it in your fave scents and you care for it. It's extremely special, after all! I really do think we should respect our homes. I cherish and respect everything I own and I feel so lucky to have it.

There is a danger of turning your house into a show home to 'impress' other people, so it's got to be about what *you* like. I browse people's homes on Instagram daily, and some of them literally take my breath away. But I don't think to myself, 'I want that house,' because I love and enjoy my own. But we can still appreciate each other's different tastes and styles. Your friend may pop over for a cuppa once a week and have a nose about, but you've got to live there day in, day out, so it's not about impressing other people, it's about being comfortable and happy in your own space.

Saying this is a big step for me, because years ago I would have decorated my home in a way that I thought other people would like or be impressed by (I'll get into that more a bit later), and it's real progress that I don't feel the need to do that any more. I honestly believe that I found myself through my home.

Is my house perfect and spotless? No way! Is it to everyone's taste? Definitely not. Some people don't like the grey and white look, so my place would be their worst nightmare because they would think it's boring. But I love it. Am I happy here? I really am.

We all have to do what suits us, and not anyone else, because sadly we do live in a world where a lot of people live their lives trying to be like someone else. Please don't! Please be you! I read a quote once that has always stuck with me. It said, 'No one is you, and that is your power.' I think that one of the worst things we can do is compare ourselves to other people. This is one of the reasons I dance around my lounge, name my cloths, put my sink to bed and show my excitement over what others may consider the most simple things, because that's just me.

Just like every person is different, so is every home, and I love that. My mum's home is full of oatmeals and browns, which I love. My friend Leanne has greens and browns, and it looks so nice. The motto for my home, however, has always been 'grey all the way'. These are mine and Jamie's four walls, and we've worked really hard saving for them, so I think we should be able to do whatever makes us happy inside them.

If you go into a shop and you love something, it doesn't matter how little it costs, what colour it is, or what other people think of it. If you take it home and you love it, then it's going to make you feel good. Colours and styles come and go all the time, so stick with what you like, and don't let anyone tell you otherwise!

Have you noticed how quickly fashions change? This includes décor. Who cares if you get a fabulous statement wall and then people decide they don't like them any more? So what? Life goes around in circles and things go in and out of style, so please yourself – you may as well, because you can't please all of the people all of the time.

Personally, I enjoy looking after things. I enjoy polishing my ornaments (with Dave, haha), karate chopping my cushions and just looking after them. I honestly think if you love your home it will love you right back.

For example, I've had the big white wooden candlestick that sits in my front room for so long now. I got it in B&M, reduced to £6.99 because the metal dish on the top had broken off. I took it home, superglued it back on, and repairing it made me smile. I gave it a new lease of life. It's been with me a long time so it's got a few chips here and there, but it still warms my heart. I could buy another one to replace it but I don't need to. Why spend money on something new when you're already happy with what you've got?

I would never leave the little Essex village I've lived in since I was young. All my friends and family still live here and it's my little bit of heaven. I've always been a home girl and if someone said to me, 'You can either have something for your wardrobe or for your home,' I'd go for home every time. It's my sanctuary, my very own box of treasures (and bargs!).

I never want to change who I am or what I buy or how I speak. I am who I am. I'm a very homely girl and my mum still comes round to help me cook. I think people believe I walk around in Louboutins, but the truth is, I don't own a pair. I think if I was ever magically given some I would end up putting them on display because I'd be so scared to wear them. I would probs Dave and Sheen them most days!

Let's face it, a lot of us are fascinated by other people's homes. I know I certainly am. I always thought it would be amazing to be an estate agent so I could have a nose around other people's places. I also really want someone to create a TV show where they go into people's houses and find out the stories behind the things they own. I bet it would be so interesting. I am actually a secret lover of shows like *Bargain Hunt* and *Antiques Roadshow*!

Every home, and every object, tells a story. I'd like to know why people have bought things and how much they were. I'd like to know about upcycling projects and how they've made them work, and find out the history of certain objects. Imagine if someone has been in their home for fifty years – their possessions would have such amazing stories to tell. I would love to sit and listen to it all!

CHAPTER TWO

HOW IT
ALL BEGAN

It's time to Hinch!

The whole Insta craziness began when Jamie and I moved into our house in July 2016. It is the first place we've owned and we saved up for it for so long. Renting and saving at the same time is so hard! I really enjoyed making our house into our home so I started taking loads of progress photos: pictures of things I'd bought and showing how I decorated each room. But I got to the stage where I felt like I was bombarding my family and friends with them.

I was worried I was posting all the time and boring people, so I set up a separate Instagram account purely for my home on

10 March 2017, and started posting photos on there instead. It was like my own little keepsake album. I actually remember feeling a little embarrassed about it at first, so I didn't tell many friends or family about it. I soon realised there were so many beautiful home accounts and I made some fabulous Insta friends; we'd take part in follow trains and boost each other's confidence with lots of lovely comments and likes. I soon became addicted to Insta! I loved it! Then one day I popped up a quick story of me cleaning my sink because I'd found a stainless steel spray (Cliff the Cif, obvs) that worked really, really well. The shine actually got me excited and that was it. I got so many DMs and it all grew from there. I still can't quite work out how it happened. If someone asked me to grow an Instagram account to this size again I wouldn't even know how to. All I do know is, be yourself and have fun every single day!

I made it very clear to everyone from day one that I'm not a professional cleaner in any way. I'm a qualified hairdresser, so that's my job and that's what I know. It's so rewarding to be able to help people feel good about themselves when they look in the mirror and smile at their new hair crown!

The hinching side of things started when the worry would kick in, or the random deep thoughts that soon led to anxious feelings inside my chest began. I would jump up, put the music channel on loud and grab the closest cloth, mop or hoover! I was no longer sitting there just thinking. Instead, I was up doing something; concentrating on something else, and before I knew it, cleaning to the beat of the music. The distraction was stopping my thoughts from running away with me and getting on top of me. I loved it, and still love it, because I feel like I'm achieving something when I clean. I like to be able to go into a room and think, 'I've done all of that.' I feel good about it, and I guess that shines through on my account.

My followers are going up in number every day and I can't really get my head around it. I'm so, so grateful but still very confused by it all! I don't often post videos of myself. I like to keep behind the scenes a lot of the time. But when *This Morning* asked me to go on the show I couldn't turn down an opportunity like that! I mean, it's one of the biggest daytime TV shows! I couldn't believe it! Those who hadn't seen me got to see what I look like for the first time. After the show was broadcast, people were like, 'Mrs Hinch revealed!' and I was honestly sat there thinking, 'How embarrassing!' I wanted the ground to swallow me up . . . whole!

OH MY GOD, I'M ON LIVE TELLY!

This Morning is the craziest thing I've ever done in my life. I would never have dreamed I'd go on a show like that. Holly and Phil are so friendly and amazing and they made me feel so relaxed.

I was really nervous the morning the show was being

recorded. I'd ordered a taxi to take me to the train station to go to London but someone at *This Morning* messaged me to say that a driver was going to pick me up. This lovely car came to my house and collected me, but when I got money out ready to give the driver at the other end he said I didn't have to pay for it. I couldn't believe it.

Jamie came to the studio with me, and thank goodness, because honestly, I just have to look at him and I'm relaxed.

I went straight in to Hair and Make-up and I knew Vanessa Feltz was there and I was like, 'What am I doing here?' I said to the hair stylist, 'You must have done some serious stars and now you're sat here doing my hair. I am sorry.' And he said he was really excited to meet me. I mean, how nice is that?

I was terrified – about people watching and then pulling me apart afterwards – but having Jamie there made all the difference. He was standing at the side of the studio as I was introduced and he gave me a thumbs up. I really wanted him to be proud of me.

I had that feeling you get before you go into an exam where your stomach is in knots and you want to eat but you can't. My biggest fear was that I might let my Hinchers down. I was so scared that I'd embarrass them. I wasn't scared of not looking my best or whatever, I just didn't want to let any-one down.

I did repeat myself a bit and I did laugh nervously a few times, but I thought for my first time on live TV I didn't do too badly. You don't have a script and you don't have time to 'rehearse', so I had to make it up as I went along. I know it was only for a few minutes but it was the scariest thing I've done in my life.

At the very end of the segment I ran off laughing and everyone was tweeting me asking me why. The fact was, my microphone was attached to the back of my bra and it started falling down and taking my actual bra with it! Can you imagine!

I felt the microphone start to go when I was cleaning the oven. I thought, 'Oh my God, I'm going to lose my bra on live TV on top of the oven.' I thought it had all finished and we'd gone to an ad break so I said to Phil, 'I nearly lost my bra, Phil!' I was holding it up and he was bent over cracking up once I explained it to him. Then Holly started laughing as well, and I ran off to try and avoid flashing anyone. At the end of the day, I got through it – live TV doesn't always go to plan, does it?

My fan pages went crazy with support. Yes, I actually have fan pages on Facebook! Can you believe it, because I can't! And it really felt like the Hinchers were a part of my extended family. Someone said they'd felt like an excited mum while they were waiting for me to go on, and other people said they were crying because they were proud to be Hinchers with me. It honestly melts my heart.

I did get some trolling, but I expected it. You can't do a massive show like that and not get some kind of criticism. Someone called me 'Essex scum', which was awful. Even though I know I don't deserve it, because I'm not hurting anyone with what I do, those things do sting.

My account just started out as a fun thing and it kind of ran away with me. All of a sudden people were using my name to advertise cleaning products, host giveaways, advertise their business, and I was getting all these emails asking me to do collaborations, promotions and shout-outs for them. It was crazy. My phone was roasting hot and my head just couldn't keep up!

I wanted to try and do it all on my own, manage it myself, but I didn't fully understand the business side of things, like legalities, briefs, contracts, etc. I knew I wanted to work with some of my favourite brands and even get merchandise out there for my Hinchers, but I had no idea how to go about it. I even tried to google everything myself!

Agencies then started contacting me and asking if I wanted them to represent me. If I'm honest, I didn't even know what that meant! I didn't know that an 'Instagram influencer' or 'Instagram talent', as they call it, was a thing! But anyway, I met with a particular management company, Gleam, and they just felt right. I mean, it felt so odd because why would I have a manager? But I felt like I needed some support so that I could concentrate on what I really loved, and that's my cleaning stories and my Instagram in general.

Being with an agency hasn't changed my Instagram because I refuse to let it; but I do feel less anxious about what to do when I'm offered working opportunities now. One day I was shining my sink and having a laugh, and the next my followers had rocketed to well over a million, and I didn't really know how to deal with it all.

THE BIG MIL!

Reaching a million followers was just amazing. My mum came round and she said to me, 'Soph, it's crazy that you've reached a million.' Then she paused and she was like, 'What exactly is it you've done, Kidda?'

I stood and thought about it and then replied, 'I don't actually know, Mum.'

A company called @lightuplovelondon had told me that if I ever hit a million followers they would send me some light-up letters to take photos with. At the time I was like, 'Nah, that's so far away.' Then one day I got 61,000 followers in a day and I was thinking, 'Hang on a minute, I reckon I can do this!'

When I hit the big million on the morning of 18 October I got so many messages my phone was red hot and I even felt slightly scared to look at the notifications.

I called @lightuplovelondon and told them when I was a few thousand off the million and they said they'd drive the letters down. I couldn't believe it. They put them in the garden and my friend Trace was lying in all sorts of positions trying to get some half-decent shots of me. She was on the ground, she was stuck to the wall, she was balancing on one leg . . . she worked hard in the garden that day!

She had to hold a chair still so I could try and climb up on to one of the letters, and it was so windy that I was blowing about all over the place. We were laughing so much, we always do. She got some fab pictures and I got 165,000 likes on the shot we used on Instagram. I couldn't believe it. I was overwhelmed that people were so happy for me. It confirmed the loyalty and the bond that I genuinely feel I have with my Hinchers.

Trace and I celebrated that night by ordering a greasy takeaway and we sat on my living room rug (yes, my pride-and-joy rug) eating cheesy spuds, burgers, pizzas and kebabs. We even popped to the shop for a cake and candles and it was one of the best days of my life.

Getting my blue tick to show my account was verified was madness too. I remember it so clearly. I was hinching my bedroom windowsill when a follower messaged me and said, 'You've done it, Mrs Hinch!' My first thought was, 'What have I done wrong?' Then she sent another message saying, 'You've got the blue tick!' YES MATE! Shut the front door! I felt like I'd been given a Blue Peter badge.

We used to get Kellogg's swim badges to sew on to our swimming costumes at primary school to show we'd passed a certain level, and I can still remember that feeling of pride when I got my first one. It was like that all over again.

I mean . . . Beyoncé's got a blue tick, mate, and now so have I. It's possibly the only thing we've got in common, but I'll take it.

'Hinching' has also made it into the Urban Dictionary. I was cracking up when someone told me and I was in total shock when I saw it. When I told Jamie he replied, 'I'm in the Urban Dictionary. Well, my surname is!' To be fair, I did congratulate him, because without his name I wouldn't be Mrs Hinch, would I!

Part of it says:

Cleaning cloths and products are very often given names which are mostly chosen by Mrs Hinch.

'I spent today hinching my home.'

Hilarious.

IT HASN'T ALL BEEN PLAIN SAILING

People who have watched my stories or read about Mrs Hinch in the press have often asked me about what happened when I ended up in hospital just before I was supposed to go on my honeymoon in 2018, so I'd like to tell you the real story.

The papers claimed it was exhaustion from appearing on *This Morning*, but that couldn't be further from the truth. My mum's side of the family has a blood condition known as Protein S deficiency, and Factor V Leiden, which is a blood disorder that causes the blood to clot, so it means I've got an increased risk of developing abnormal blood clots.

I knew I had this blood disorder mildly from tests I'd had in my early teens, but they didn't think it was that bad. I didn't even need medication at the time I was tested. But then one day I got a strange pain in my lower back so I went to see a chiropractor. It wasn't easing up, and they couldn't work out why I had this pain.

A few days later I went to open a new Savers store in Witham, Essex, and so many Hinchers came along it was amazing – I still can't thank you enough for taking the time to come and see me.

We were having so much fun taking lots of pictures and I was even signing bottles of Zoflora! But after an hour I felt like I needed to sit down. The pain in my back and left leg brought me close to tears, but I thought to myself, 'What if they think I think I'm too posh to stand?' so I tried my best to stay on my feet for longer.

All of a sudden I said to Jamie, 'My leg's gone dead. I can't feel it,' so I sat down and stretched it out in front of me and it was about four times the size of my right leg. Funnily enough, that's when I knew something wasn't quite right!

I went back to Tracy's house as it was only round the corner, and she called an ambulance. I went to my local hospital in Chelmsford where they did a full body scan and as soon as they got the results they put me in an ambulance and blue lighted me up to St Thomas's in London. I remember being really frightened of losing my leg.

Rather than having a bad back, it turned out I actually had a large blood clot in my iliac vein. I was diagnosed with MTS (May-Thurner syndrome) along with the Protein S deficiency and Factor V Leiden. The doctors put me on IV blood thinners immediately but the clot wasn't dispersing. My leg was getting bigger and they were worried, so they had to operate.

I had two little operations down in theatre where they gave me a clot buster treatment and also cleverly fitted three stents to keep the iliac vein open.

I was in hospital for over a week in the end and I was a little bit underweight from being ill (also, when I'm nervous the weight drops off), so they fed me up and said I needed to gain weight before I was able to leave. It really was a terrible week but the hospital couldn't have been kinder to me.

It was such a strange time as my account was really taking off, and because I'd been on *This Morning* just before I was admitted, the story ended up in the papers. I couldn't believe it! Reading incorrect stories about yourself is the most frustrating feeling!

One night on the ward the lights were switched off and I just burst into tears. My phone notifications were flashing like mad and I thought, 'What is happening here? What is going on? Why are people writing about me in the papers?' It was so mad. I also missed hinching so much because it helps me to keep my mind focused, and I'm not joking, to not be able to dust with Dave or mop with Vera was tough! I looked forward to the ward cleaner coming to mop around my bed every day! We had a giggle.

In the end I sat up in bed with the baby wipes my mum had brought in for me and I cleaned the little wooden table that goes over the bed until the packet was nearly empty, just to make myself feel better.

My mind was going round and round, so another thing I did to keep myself calm was to section out a tube of Smarties someone had brought me into different colour groups. That showed me how much I needed to hinch. My mind was doing somersaults.

It was so nice when I was able to come home and cuddle my dog Henry again and smell my own home. I am now on blood thinners for life, but I was so lucky with the brilliant treatment I received and I feel incredibly blessed. To all the staff who helped me, I thank you. I will be forever grateful.

MY GOALS FOR THE NEAR FUTURE

My aims are to improve my cooking skills and to learn another language. I really enjoyed GCSE French at school and I would love to be able to speak it fluently.

Jamie and I are also planning our house extension, which is a big thing for us. We'd like more space if our family is going to grow. There's bound to be a lot of dust and mess everywhere, which will need a lot of hinching, but it's going to be so worth it!

The way I'll keep myself relaxed will be to keep all the rooms I can keep clean and tidy as nice as they possibly can look. It will be challenging, but also a really good lesson in letting go for me. There is going to be mess no matter how much I hinch, and I have to accept that. Sharon Shark will be going ten to the dozen during that time, bless her.

Our plan is to have a dining room added, our lounge is going to be extended and I'm hoping I'll be able to have a fireplace fitted somewhere in the extension. I've always wanted one. I find them so cosy.

Upstairs we're going to have two double bedrooms, one with an en suite and one with large fitted wardrobes. I've only got one wardrobe at the moment which I share with Mr Hinch, so a lot of my clothes are stored in drawers. As you may already know, some of them are in Henry's room, and that just won't do. I'm sure he has more clothes than I do.

A couple of people have said to me that it would be easier for us to buy a bigger house but this is where I feel happiest. Nothing will beat how I feel in this house. It's our home and it's brought us so much joy. It's not about moving to somewhere bigger and 'better'. To me there is nowhere better than where we are right now.

Not surprisingly, I plan to do it all on a budget and I would love my Hinchers to get involved in our house extension journey. It would be amazing if they let me know if they spot anything 'Mrs Hinch style' that may look good in the new part of our house. I'll be flagging up what I'm looking for, and then if anyone is out and about and they see something that might work they can let me know. I want us all to do this together.

I've never done anything like this before. I've never started from scratch and had the opportunity to create something totally new, so I'm really looking forward to it.

As for long-term plans, it's all about family for me. I love being a wife to Jamie. Being a mum will be a dream come true. And a good cook? Well, that would just be a bonus! I'm so excited about having mini Hinchers running around the place.

It's always good to have goals and I find writing mine down helps me to focus on what I want. I've whipped up this page for you to fill in so you can do the same. Crystal pens at the ready, Hinchers!

DIARY

_____

○ What hobby would you like to take up?

....

....

....

○ What home improvements would you like to make?

....

....

....

○ What would you love to buy for your house?

....

....

....

○ What's your best cleaning tip?

....

....

....

○ What are your top five cleaning products?

1) ....

2) ....

3) ....

4) ....

5) ....

○ What makes your house feel like a home?

....

....

....

PART TWO
Welcome To My Hinching World

CHAPTER THREE

HINCHIONARY

Yes mate!

MINKEH

THE STORIES BEHIND SOME OF MY FAVOURITE WORDS AND SAYINGS

All the Best

When Jamie and I worked together in London, it was something that was always said around the office. Everyone used to jokingly say 'all the best' as in 'good luck with that'.

It really made me laugh and Jamie and I started saying it to each other at home when either of us said something wrong or funny. I said it on my stories a couple of times without even thinking about it and my followers started saying it too. It's become such a strong part of my vocab that I honestly don't even realise I'm saying it half the time. So all the best to that!

Bargs

Barg is such a classic Essex thing to say and obviously short for 'bargain'. A lot of words are shortened in the town where I live, like jealous is jel and emotional is emosh. Bargs has been around for a long time, so I've said it for ages.

Hinch Hauls

Hinch hauls are basically whatever I come home with after I've been out shopping for bargs. When I get home I show everyone what I've bought, whether it's cleaning products, clothes, food or a new basket.

People seem to really enjoy the hinch haul stories, and it means I feel slightly less guilty about all the shopping I do! I personally love seeing what people pick up when they go shopping!

Hinching

I couldn't call my account 'Mrs Hinchliffe Home' because it was too long, and my maiden name didn't have the right ring to it. Mrs Hinch Home just flowed.

I wasn't married to Jamie when I set up my account but I was engaged and I knew I was going to be Mrs Hinchliffe one day, so I decided I could get away with it.

One day in passing I said that I'd 'hinched' something while I was cleaning and that was it. It's all been organic and has happened naturally. I didn't ever sit down and think, 'Right, I need to create some kind of slogan.' I didn't think that far ahead so it didn't even cross my mind.

One day someone said they were a 'Hincher', so all of my followers became my Hinchers and #hinching became a thing. Then Hinchmas and everything else said so lightheartedly just followed. I'm lucky I've got a surname that seems to work so well with everything!

I Love a Barg

I love bargains and I love sniffing out something that looks like it should be much more expensive. I think people assume I get everything for free but I really don't. I'm always on the lookout for a bargain rug or lamp when I'm doing my hauls. I feel a real sense of achievement when I find something that looks like it should be ten times the price.

My family are not materialistic in any way, nor are they into designer labels. If someone said to me, 'Here's a lamp that is £500 and here's one that's £5,' if I genuinely preferred the £5 lamp, then that's the one I would go for. One of my favourite lamps cost me £9.99 from B&M. Now that is a barg!

I love all of the home accounts on Instagram and I've got so much respect for the people that run them. A lot of the accounts helped me to find some lovely things for my house by searching hashtags. For instance, I searched #greyinteriors (shock) and #interiordesign and they brought up so many dreamy images. I've searched for all sorts – #loungegoals, #silversofas, you name it. That's the beauty of Instagram. It's a never-ending source of ideas.

When we put the deposit down on our house the first thing I did was go on Pinterest and take screenshots of things I loved so I could save them and use them as inspiration. It's taken a while, especially as when we moved in we hardly had any money left in the bank, but it doesn't all have to be done overnight. And it's all come together now.

I upcycled furniture to save money. For instance, the ottoman in my lounge, which I can never get rid of because I love it, was from a boot sale. I took all the nails out of the top (mission mate) and painted it with Wilko's own-brand paint. Then I ordered some fabric from eBay and re-covered the seat and even made a cushion to match (with a bit of help from my sister's mother-in-law, Sandra). It makes it feel really personal and you end up getting really attached to things that you've put a lot of time and effort into. Well, I do, anyway!

I also love boot sales and the boot sale apps Shpock, Gumtree and Facebook Marketplace. You can get such great bargs and sometimes you can see potential in things that other people don't.

They say one person's trash is another person's treasure, and I completely agree! One hundred people may walk past a piece of furniture and not give it a second glance, but it could catch your eye and you'll fall in love with it on the spot. As soon as I saw that ottoman looking a bit old and sad I knew it needed to be 'hinched' and I could bring it back to life.

You have to look at something with love to see its potential. Ignore the odd broken bit because things can be fixed, and don't worry about the colour or the dodgy material because that can easily be changed.

Don't worry about how cheap it is either. I paid pennies for my ottoman and it's one of the best things I own. I've been offered expensive new ones but I feel happy every time I look at that one, so why would I want another? When I see people sitting on my ottoman I feel so proud. And can I just mention that the glass table next to it was a bargain too? I got it from Shpock and it only cost me £20, but they're a fortune in the shops.

I've always shopped in bargain shops. It all started with toiletries when I was growing up. I never understood why people spent a fortune on shower gel when they're all the same to me. It's nice to treat yourself sometimes, but some of the products that cost £1 smell so amazing and I loved testing them out.

People always ask me what my favourite shops are and they're all high-street stores that you can find in most towns, like B&M, Poundstretcher, Poundland, The Range, Home Bargains, Savers and Wilko, to name a few.

Nothing makes me happier than going down the cleaning aisle of a shop, but the problem is that half the time I'll come home with bags full of cleaning products and no food. I'll be like, 'Well, I've got some Zoflora but where are the eggs?' I get very easily distracted.

My Mate Minkeh

A Minkeh (or the Minky Antibacterial Cleaning Pad, to give it its official name) is basically a cleaning must-have that I am in love with. I'm not ashamed of it, I love all of my cloths, but Minkeh has a very special place in my heart.

The name Minkeh came about because my dad is actually Northern so I say it in his accent. Every time I say it I think of him.

I first used Minkeh when I saw another cleaning account using it on her stories. I messaged her and asked, 'What is that green sponge that you're using, please?' She was super friendly and when she replied I ordered one straight away on eBay. As soon as I tested him out on my bath . . . I fell in love.

I got genuinely attached to Minkeh because I was using him every day and he made whatever job I was doing easier, and that bit more fun! I'd finish a job and then look at Minkeh and think, 'Yes, mate, we did it, we're a team.' Sometimes it would just be me and him together for hours a day, cleaning.

I have become so attached to Minkeh that when I was in Poundstretcher looking for a couple of bargs and I came across an Elf on the Shelf bathrobe, I was like, 'Hang on a minute, that looks like it would fit Minkeh perfectly.' And I was right! As soon as I put it on him that was it, I was straight online ordering him some more clothes. Now please don't worry; it was all a light-hearted joke, and still is to this day! I understand Minkeh doesn't have a beating heart in that white belly of his! (Or does he? Who knows.)

It started as a complete laugh but people absolutely loved it and started saying, 'It's not Elf on the Shelf any more, it's Mink on the Sink.'

The hashtag #minkonthesink kicked off and then tons of other people started dressing their Minkehs up and putting them in different scenarios, so they were hanging out all over the house wearing different clothes.

I know Elf on the Shelf is for kids at Christmas, but I can't imagine there are many parents who don't really enjoy using their imagination to create funny photos too. I love setting up little scenarios in my mind and doing things in a cute way that makes people smile.

One lady recorded a little video of her daughter who was about to turn six. She said, 'What have you asked for for your birthday?' and she replied, 'A Minkeh, Mum!' It was the sweetest thing. This little girl didn't want toys, she just wanted a Minkeh to dress up. That made me so happy.

The thing is, we can all feel like we're kids at times and maybe I feel like that more than some. When the younger family members are around they have these dolls that are so advanced it's quite scary. I find myself putting nappies on them or feeding them with a bottle when they're crying. They'll ask for them back and I'm a bit like, 'Already?'

Anyway, back to Minkeh. Things went so crazy that the Hinchers crashed the Minky website. They sold out everywhere in the UK and people started buying in bulk and attempting to sell them for small fortunes on eBay.

I really tried to stop people buying overpriced Minkehs because there will always be more made and sold at the original price. It's that thing of wanting something there and then, and I totally get that, but the cloths will work just as well when they're back in stock. It's sad that people try and 'take the Minkeh' but I guess that's just the way things are at times.

That's not the only time this sort of thing has happened. In fact, Hinchers are so loyal they're known as 'the website crashers' online because as soon as they see something they like on my stories they're off!

I really believe in Minky's products and so many people thought I was sponsored by them for so long, but I honestly wasn't. I started using the cloths on my stories when I only had a couple of thousand followers so they definitely weren't paying me to use it. Minkeh has become a lifelong friend. If I like something, I'll share it, and if I don't . . . I won't! Simple as that.

Narnia

Anyone who has watched my stories will know all about Narnia. It's my pride and joy and it's (sort of) helped me to achieve the dream I've had since I was a kid of having my own shop.

Narnia came about because one day I'd been on a hinch haul. I'd bought some cleaning products and when I got home I couldn't physically fit them in the house because my cleaning cupboard was bursting at the seams. I was doing an Insta live and I went into my garage and discovered a white wardrobe that was full of old suits and coats I was planning to sell at a boot sale but had never got around to.

I took everything out of the wardrobe and then hung all of my spray bottles on the rail at the top. Next I hung a Velcro shoe rack alongside them and filled it with all of my new products. I even put fairy lights around it to make it look pretty because I was so happy to have somewhere to store everything.

Jamie was at the gym at the time and I knew there was no way he could have gone in there and seen it, so I was joking to everyone that I'd get away with it. I was laughing with everyone about the fact that he was due home and I was scared he was going to discover what I'd done. When he did finally spot it he said to me, 'Oh my God, babe, it's like Narnia in there.' That name has stuck ever since and it suits it perfectly – a never-ending cupboard of magic.

One day I decided to take things a step further so I bought some storage boxes and spent ages assembling them. But as soon as I had put them together they all collapsed and it was carnage. My parents just so happened to turn up for a cuppa, because they like to randomly do that sometimes, and I could see from my dad's face that he felt really sorry for me. He came round the following week and put up wooden shelves inside my wardrobe so I could put everything in there neatly – it was like all my Christmases had come at once.

The wardrobe cost around £100 from Ikea years ago and I've been offered some amazing storage units through my account now, but I can't detach myself from this particular wardrobe. It's been with me every step of the way and I would feel so guilty if I replaced it with a newer model. How harsh would that be? I created it, Jamie named it and my dad rebuilt it, and I'll never chuck it out because it's become a big part of the hinching journey.

I do have a lot of products in that cupboard and people take the mickey out of me about it all the time, but it means I never have to go out to the shops just to get one thing. I go shopping in my Narnia instead. I would be devastated if they discontinued something I love so I always have a couple spare. It's nice to know they're always there.

I keep a couple of bags out there and I'll fill them up with whatever I need and bring it all inside. It's my go-to place and I know I'll always be able to do a wash or polish. If I run low, I'll replace it. My stocks are constantly being replenished.

I also keep things like loo rolls, Henry's treats and

medication in there. It's dry and safe and I can get to what I need easily. I know not everyone can have a Narnia and I'm really lucky to have the space for it in my garage, but you don't have to have storage that's as big as mine. You can stock up any unused cupboard and buy second-hand wardrobes or chests of drawers for so little from Shpock or Facebook Marketplace. And if you've got a garage or a space for a Narnia of your own somewhere there's nothing to stop you.

It makes me feel calm when I look at my Narnia because everything is neat and has its rightful home. Some people collect stamps or china dolls, I collect cleaning products and cloths!

Where's It From?

Everything in my house was a barg. On the following pages are the things I get asked about most, and where they're from, so you can see you don't have to splash the cash to make your home look lovely.

MY BEST BARGS

Baskets . . .

Belly basket
@our_littlegreyhome

Shopping style with handles
Poundstretcher

Stickers for my studio style baskets
@binkyboodesigns

Studio style
@whamworld

o

Bed
@loveliving

o

Bedding
eBay, Next, Matalan or Christy

o

Framed perfume bottles
*I bought some empty bottles from eBay
and I framed them. They cost hardly
anything but people love them*

o

Grey-and-white striped bedroom cushions
HomeSense

o

Kitchen trolley
Ikea

o

Large lanterns in the living room
B&M

o

Large prints around my home
@desenio

o

Large wall mirror behind my sofa
Furniture Village

o

Large white wicker heart
@charlestedinteriors

o

Light switch covers
eBay

o

Lounge curtains
Kylie Minogue range in Oyster

o

Love-heart in kitchen
Facebook Marketplace for £20

o

Radiator covers
eBay

o

Rug
@therugseller

o

Silver mirror in my hallway
@williamwoodmirrors

o

Silver vase/candle tray
eBay

o

Tea, Coffee and Sugar canisters
@handmade_at_herbert_cottage

o

TV cabinet
Ikea

o

White fur pompom
bedroom cushions
TK Maxx

o

I bought my first belly basket via an account on Instagram last year. When I went to buy a bigger one, the lady who runs the account said she'd send it to me for free because my numbers were going up so much and I had sent so much business her way. She messaged me the following week to say again she couldn't believe how much her sales had gone up because I'd featured her product on my account.

The same thing happened with Ava May Aromas. Hannah, the lady who owns the business, sent me a very emotional letter to say that I had changed her life. She now has a workshop and ten-plus employees working all hours under the sun. I love that her business is doing so well!

There's nothing I love more than coming home, getting a blanket out of my belly basket and lighting a wax melt. I think it's because when I was growing up, if I wasn't feeling good, my mum would always say to me, 'Go and get your blanket, get comfy on the sofa and watch telly.' It still chills me out. I am also the proud owner of a large stuffed yellow and brown clock called 'cuddle clock'. I've had him since I was born, and he is still with me to this day.

CHAPTER FOUR

IT'S TOTALLY NORMAL TO NAME YOUR CLOTHS

Dave the Duster

've been naming my cleaning products for a long time now, and people may think I'm mad, but that's fine!

It all started when I was using my yellow cloth one day to shine my sink. I remember cleaning the sink and telling people on my story how fab my cloth was and how I was really attached to it. I joked and decided to give it a name and a follower messaged me and said, 'Mrs Hinch, call it Buddy.' I did think of it as my buddy so it worked well and it went on from there.

People started messaging me saying, 'Where's that yellow

cloth from?' and I'd reply, 'Oh, you mean Buddy?' People got used to it and they seemed to really get into it.

Before I knew it, I was being tagged in pictures of Hinchers with their buddies and it was heart-warming for me. This is when the connection I have with my Hinchers began.

My cloths are like a family to me and they've all got their own individual personalities. Thankfully they all get on really well and are happy to work together. All the best!

Since the cloth family formed, some of my appliances and cleaning products have also got in on the action, like Sharon the Shark, Dave the Duster and Vera the Vileda mop.

This is the latest list, but it's growing all the time as I try and love new things. You know a product has to be something really special, though, to make it into the family!

THE HINCHING FAMILY

- Barry Brushes

- Buddy and Brian Spontex Kitchen Cloths

- Buff Tings Mop Slippers

- Clarence the Polish Cloth (my niece Abi named that for me, bless her)

- Cliff the Cif Stainless Steel Spray

- Dave the Pledge Fluffy Duster
- Derek the Dishmatic
- Elvis Elbow Grease
- Gregory Gloves
- Kermit the Green Minky Window and Glass Cloth
- Lennie the Lint Roller
- Minkeh! (the original and best)
- Neil the Kneeling Pad
- Paul the Pine-Scented Disinfectant
- Pinkeh Moppet Sponge
- Sharon the Shark Hoover
- Shelley the Handheld Shark Hoover
- Stewart the SonicScrubber
- Trace the Turbo Mop
- Vera the Vileda Spray Mop
- Victor the Vileda Windowmatic Vacuum (he's pretty posh)

THE CLEANING THINGS
I CAN'T LIVE WITHOUT

To me, a cupboard full of hinching products is absolute heaven, and, boy, do they keep me occupied! When I need to hinch my house, there's my team right there!

The Products

1001 CARPET FRESH SPRAY

Thai Orchid and Passion Fruit is my absolute favourite smell in the 1001 range. It's gorgeous. This stuff is magic on rugs and carpets. The great thing is that you can just spray it on and leave it, you don't need to hoover it up. It's a quick and easy daily freshen up, especially if you have pets in your home.

ACE STAIN REMOVER AND COLOUR BRIGHTENER

I really rate this, and it's cheap as chips. Pop a capful in the washing machine drum and it's as simple as that.

ARIEL GEL

I love this because it has the Febreze technology in it, and that is a game changer. It works really well and it's like a reliable old friend.

I've tried using the washing pods because they seem really easy to just chuck in the machine, but several times I took my washing out to find the melted plastic bit stuck to a pair of jeans or a top, so they had to go back in and be washed again. Also, the smell wasn't strong enough for me. I am not a fan of quick fixes if they cause more work!

ASTONISH MOULD AND MILDEW BLASTER
Coupled up with Minkeh, this stuff works miracles in the bathroom. My tile grout has never looked so new.

ASTONISH OXY ACTIVE PLUS
This is another product I love for washing. I always put a scoop into the drawer of my washing machine. It's a stain remover but I think it makes all my clothes look much brighter.

ASTONISH SPECIALIST HOB AND COOKTOP CLEANER AND SPONGE
It comes with its own sponge and it's got that chalky texture that can set your teeth on edge a bit, but it does a brilliant job of getting off any tough stains.

ASTONISH WINDOW AND GLASS CLEANER SPRAY
I am yet to find a glass cleaner that can top this! I spray all my mirrored furniture and my windows with this! I then wipe away with Kermit (Minky window and glass cloth) and the magic is done!

BAR KEEPERS FRIEND

I love this but it's very strong, so you need to be careful with how long you leave it on stainless steel so it doesn't strip it. It's amazing stuff but it does try and eat away at your sink if you leave it for too long.

Some products are very strong, which is why they're so effective, but always read the labels to ensure you use them correctly.

BICARBONATE OF SODA

This is such a magic product and so cheap to buy. You can get a big box of it for around £1.50, which is nothing considering how long it lasts.

Bicarbonate of soda is extremely versatile and has many useful properties.

Try it as a mild abrasive or scouring agent on shiny materials, as it can clean without scratching. It is suitable for use on aluminium, chrome, jewellery, plastic, porcelain, silver, stainless steel and tin.

Bicarbonate of soda is a fab deodoriser and it can be used in the refrigerator, on carpets, upholstery, vinyl, and in bins and drains.

TOP TIP:

- Pour some bicarb into a small organza bag and 'hide' in a convenient location to help keep odours at bay. Also ideal for wardrobes and drawers to stop clothes smelling musty.

- Leave some in an open container in the fridge. Once the deodorising effect is wearing off, pour it down the kitchen sink to help keep the drain clean and fresh.
- Also leave a small dish sat in the microwave when switched off to eliminate odours.

BLOO FOAM AROMA

All you do is pour a capful down the toilet and your loo will fizz up and smell amazing. Simple. It's best left overnight to work its magic!

TOP TIP: If you pour it from higher up it will fizz up more.

CIF CREAM ORIGINAL WITH MICRO CRYSTALS

I really rate this for the hob and sink. I always use it with Minkeh because it makes it more effective and yes, I find it fun to use! Who can't resist writing 'hinched' on their cooker? I certainly can't. This also works really well on all PVC.

CIF PERFECT FINISH STAINLESS STEEL SPRAY

Oh, Cliff. Cliff! He's such a gentleman. Cliff and Buddy are one hundred percent best mates. I use this team on my sink every single day without fail! The shine is simply beautiful!

CIF POWER AND SHINE MULTI-PURPOSE WIPES

These are by far my number one must-have wipes. One wipe works so well and smells so fresh! I use them to clean the toilets, my remote controls, door handles and even shoes. They disinfect and make things look super clean in no time at all. I hate to use this word because I dislike it as much as everyone, but they really are the perfect amount of moist (haha! Sorry!).

DETTOL ALL IN ONE SPRAY

This claims to kill flu and cold viruses, so I'm sold. It's safe to use on pet beds, too, so it's an all-round must-have. It also smells so clean and fresh! I have so many cans of it in my Narnia.

DP SODA CRYSTALS

I get mine from Morrisons, once again, £1 a bag! I use this on plugs, drains and my washing machine!

Soda crystals are a great water softener, as well as ideal for tackling dirt, grease and oil.

Use soda crystals in and around the home for:

- Cleaning and deodorising the washing machine
- Removing burnt-on residue on pots and pans
- Helping to keep sinks and drains fresh and blockage-free
- Grease removal in household cleaning and laundry

- Removing moss and algae from paths and patios
- Cleaning toilets as an alternative to common cleaners
- Cleaning silver jewellery

DR BECKMANN CARPET STAIN REMOVER

It's the one. It's the *only* one. I love that the brush comes attached to the bottle! Super easy and quick to use.

ELBOW GREASE

Aka Elvis. He does the work so you don't have to! (Okay, you may still have to do a bit.) This stuff is incredible for everything. I've even used it on clothes stains before. I sprayed it directly on to the stain, popped it into the washing machine and it came out a treat. It's a multipurpose cleaner that can be used on practically everything.

FAIRY LIQUID

I've always used Fairy and I don't think you can beat it. I was sent a personalised Mrs Hinch Fairy Liquid bottle on 5 October 2018. The date is etched on my mind because it was like winning the World Cup for me. What a day!

FLASH ANTI-BACTERIAL FLOOR WIPES

If you don't have time to get your mop out and do your floors, these work wonders. I've got laminate flooring but they work for most floor types.

FLASH BATHROOM SPRAY

You can't beat this. The suds are amazing and it also has the Febreze technology in it so it's a double whammy. It breaks down all soap and scum, and the shine is fabulous. Coupled up with Minkeh you can't beat this duo. I've always said if I could wear Flash Bathroom as a perfume, I would . . . and I am not joking! This spray is used in my bathrooms, sinks, showers, baths . . . Everywhere!

HARPIC ACTIVE FRESH MOUNTAIN PINE TOILET CLEANER

My absolute angel! I'm in love with this. It's got a perfect pine scent, which makes me feel Christmassy all year round, and the smell lingers for hours!

LENOR FABRIC CONDITIONER

I love this one because it doesn't irritate my skin and the smell is divine. My fave scent is Spring Awakening. I also dilute this fabric conditioner with water to wipe down all the painted woodwork in my house, from skirting boards to door frames and banisters! Minkeh obviously joins in on this!

LENOR SPRING AWAKENING TUMBLE DRYER SHEETS

These are such a bargain and they're multi-taskers so I use them for loads of things. They're anti-static so they're especially brilliant for picking up pet hair and dust.

I use a tumble sheet to clean my blinds and to clean the

dainty crystals on my chandeliers. I also pop them inside all my cushion covers and pillowcases, under the sofa seat cushions, and between clothes when packing a suitcase to keep it all smelling beaut!

LENOR UNSTOPPABLES FRESH IN-WASH SCENT BOOSTERS

I use these in every wash, they are a dream. I also create my own little scent bags by popping some into an organza bag and hanging them in my car, airing cupboard or wardrobe. I also keep one inside Mr Hinch's gym bag. No wonder he smells so good! Haha!

MR SHEEN MULTI-SURFACE POLISH

This is a whizz for glass, metal, wood, plastic – anything goes. I use it with a classic old-school yellow duster cloth (Clarence) and this never lets me down.

PINE-SCENTED DISINFECTANT (STARDROPS OR ASTONISH)

My amazing Paul the Pine. It's so cheap and it works so well and smells absolutely amazing to me.

PLEDGE ELECTRONICS WIPES

Safe for your electronics and work so well. It shocks me that people still use wet wipes on their TV, which could do it real damage. I'd be devastated if my TV was injured!

STARDROPS LEATHER CLEAN AND FEED

I'll spray this on my armchair if I feel like it needs a bit of a treat, teamed up with Pinkeh. It's a fairly new discovery for me but it's brilliant and the chair laps it up. I also use this product to clean the leather interior of my car, as well as my leather shoes – restores the shine. Best leather cleaner I've used yet.

THE PINK STUFF

They call it the miracle cleaning paste, and yes it is. It's unreal. I mainly use it on the base of my pots and pans, tile grouting, oven, hob, ceramic sinks and ornaments. It does a cracking job and never lets me down.

TOILET DUCK FRESH DISCS IN MARINE

I'm not going to lie, I really enjoy using the little applicator to stick them on the inside of my toilet because it makes me feel a bit excited when it comes out perfectly round. I'm easily pleased. Also the Toilet Duck pine strips that peel off smell unreal!

VIAKAL

You need this in your life. It's strong, so make sure you only leave it on for the recommended time. I spray it on the shower doors, shower heads, taps, etc. It's a magical limescale remover for me and it also leaves a fabulous shine. I leave it for a maximum of five minutes before I rinse it off.

ZOFLORA (ONE OF MY LIFE'S LOVES)

As everyone knows, I love Zoflora and Springtime is my number one, closely followed by Mountain Air, Lavender Escape, Country Garden and Linen Fresh.

I love to use Mountain Air on my floors because it's stronger, and, like all Zoflora disinfectants, it's also pet friendly when diluted correctly. Always remember to leave the floors to dry before allowing your pets back on them and carefully follow the usage instructions.

I also like to use Linen Fresh Zoflora in my washing machine when I wash my towels and bath mats! The smell reminds me of my mum as it's her favourite Zoflora.

I have so many spray bottles labelled with my top Zofloras. It's just an amazing product, with many uses, and from £1 a bottle you can't go wrong! Here are my favourite ways to use Zoflora:

TOP TIP: Always carry out a patch test on an inconspicuous area before using Zoflora.

BASKETS AND CAGES

Zoflora is safe to use in your pets' baskets, kennels, hutches and cages to hygienically clean these areas, eliminating any pet-related bacteria and odours. Allow to dry before returning pets to the area. Add Zoflora to a spray bottle containing water, spray directly on to the area and wipe over with a cloth of your choice. You can also use it to clean your pet's toys: simply dilute your chosen Zoflora with water and soak plastic chew toys in the solution to be thoroughly disinfected. Rinse thoroughly with clean water and allow to dry BEFORE returning to your pet.

BIN

To ensure your bin is germ-free and smells nice, soak a cloth in diluted Zoflora and wipe it out, not forgetting the lid and surrounding areas, inside and out. Also keep your bin fresh-smelling for longer by diluting your favourite Zoflora disinfectant in a trigger spray containing water, then spray directly on to the rubbish in the bin. You can even soak some kitchen roll in Zoflora and pop it in the bottom of your bin, before adding the bag, and leave it there for extra freshness.

CARPETS AND RUGS

If you have a pet in the home, mix up a mop bucket of diluted Zoflora, and after vacuuming the carpets, use a clean mop dipped in the Zoflora solution (and wrung out) to gently mop the carpet surface. It lifts the pile and keeps the house smelling fresh and fragrant.

CLEANING CLOTHS AND SPONGES

Dilute Zoflora in water in the sink and leave your dish-cloths to soak. It's good practice to do this at the end of every day, then by the next morning your whole kitchen will be fresh-smelling and your dishcloths hygienic for each day's use. This is what I refer to as 'putting the babies to bed'.

CLOTH AND BUCKET

Tackle surfaces around the home from the kitchen to the bedroom using a cloth of choice and a bucket of water. For best results, remove heavy soiling first then wipe away the bacteria using Zoflora. But remember, Zoflora should not come into contact with polished wood. With soft furnishings, always check for colour fastness first.

Dilute the recommended amount of Zoflora for the amount of water you're using. Protect your hands from all your hard work by using rubber Gregory Gloves, and always wash your hands after use.

DRAINS AND TOILETS

Use Zoflora straight from the bottle to fight nasty odours caused by bacteria in your drains and plugholes. Or give your toilet bowl an injection of bacteria-busting fragrance and disinfect your toilet brush at the same time. Use a capful of Zoflora in bacteria-concentrated areas such as drains and toilet-brush holders. Remember, Zoflora is flammable when not diluted so do not expose it to open flames or apply direct heat.

FLOORING

I add diluted Zoflora directly to my trigger spray mop, aka Vera, which is fab for those quick everyday floor hinches!

But for a more thorough clean, add Zoflora to a mop bucket of water, aka Trace, and use it to mop over hard floor surfaces. If floors are muddy or greasy, they will need to be cleaned first with a floor-cleaning product before disinfecting with Zoflora. I personally love to use the Flash floor cleaner.

WORKTOPS

Dilute your favourite Zoflora fragrance into a spray bottle containing water, then spray directly on to the area and wipe over with a cloth (I love Pinkeh for this!). The Zoflora fragrances will eliminate any cooking odours and freshen the whole room. (Not suitable for areas in direct contact with food, such as chopping boards, as the perfume may cause tainting.)

Zoflora is one of my absolute favourite products because you can pick and choose the different scents and I'm secretly addicted to collecting them! But also it's because you can use it on almost anything! Use it to disinfect your bath and showers, your cupboard handles, light switches, remote controls, radiators and even your phone! But remember the only surface that must be avoided is polished wood.

The Tools

BIN BAGS

I use heavy-duty large black bags with handles because I find the drawstrings break easily. The heavy-duty kind are best.

Mr Hinch is very particular about the bin bags so he doesn't like it if I buy the wrong ones! I leave the bin and bin bags as his domain!

DISHMATIC

I have about ten of these Derek Dishmatics. You can use them all around the home. I use them primarily for washing up, so it's always quick and easy as they're loaded with Fairy and ready to go. I also fill one with Flash Bathroom Liquid and use it to scrub away at my shower tray and bathroom tiles. Derek just gets the job done!

DUST MOP SLIPPERS

These make me laugh so much, but they do actually work really well too! I ordered them as a joke from eBay because I was always too scared to walk on my kitchen floor after I'd washed it in case I got footprints on it.

A few of my followers told me about mop slippers so I ordered a pair and when I put them on my feet I thought they were buff tings, so that's what they were christened.

EXTRA THICK MOPPETS

Pinkeh! As we know, sponges don't have to be pink to be called Pinkeh. It's a universal term for a moppet-type sponge. I use Pinkeh on all worktops, my dining table, leather arm-chairs and the leather seats in my car. Teamed up with my diluted Zoflora spray, I'm in heaven!

HEAVY-DUTY SCRUBBING BRUSH

Aka Barry! Basically, bargain hard-bristled hand-held brushes. I use these for my rug, and to brush away annoying mud on the carpet (make sure you leave the mud to dry first – never try and wipe it away wet).

KNEELING PAD

Neil! He's actually a gardener's kneeling pad but is so brilliant to use around the house to save your poor knees when hinching floors or skirtings. I bought mine for £2 in Poundstretcher.

LINT CLOTHES BRUSH

My nan used to have one of these red clothes brushes when I was growing up and they are genius for picking up any kind of hair, especially pet hair, from the sofa. It's the quickest way to give your sofa a five-minute hinch! Finish off with a spray of Febreze. Job's a good 'un!

MINKY ANTI-BACTERIAL CLEANING PAD

Minkeh needs no introduction. I can't do without my Minkehs. I use the white belly side on woodwork and doors, etc, as it's more of a scourer-type texture. I then use the green honeycomb side to wipe away any suds or remaining product to finish off the job.

MINKY GLASS AND WINDOW CLOTH
Kermit is a wonder. He's a brilliant buffer on any shiny surface. Give him a try and you'll see for yourself.

NO MORE NAILS / COMMAND ADHESIVE HOOKS
I love hooks. I would have a hook for everything if I could. I love to hang my cloths on them. No More Nails / Command Hooks and Command Hanging Strips are amazing.

No More Nails is such a gift for me because it's so straightforward. Anything that doesn't involve a hammer and nails is such a bonus. I always feel like a total DIY whizz when I've put up a picture or something. I honestly think I've got a future as a handywoman (that's such a lie).

PLEDGE FLUFFY DUSTER
Dave!!! Who doesn't love Dave! I'll use him to dust off all of my surfaces before I Mr Sheen them. He works brilliantly and traps the dust really well instead of just moving it around. You can buy replacement heads for him which means he is reusable time and time again. A strong member of the Hinch family!

RUBBER GLOVES
Always wear your Gregorys. I have got better but I don't wear them nearly enough, which is a nightmare when you have long nails like I do! But of course I do really recommend them, especially when you're dealing with harsh chemicals.

SHARK CORDLESS HANDHELD VACUUM CLEANER

Shelley! I use her all the time for getting rid of worktop crumbs and giving the car interior a quick hinch. She may be small but don't be fooled, she is powerful and so convenient!

SHARK DUOCLEAN CORDLESS UPRIGHT VACUUM WITH POWERED LIFT-AWAY

My Sharon! I've had every hoover going over the years. My mum gave me her old Dyson and I absolutely loved it, but when it finally packed up someone mentioned the Shark to me and I thought, 'Yeah, but it's not a Dyson.' Then I tried it, and oh my God, the hoover lines you get are a thing of beauty.

You do need a powerful hoover to create hoover lines, but they're not hard to do. I've hoovered words into my carpet and all sorts (don't ask)!

SONICSCRUBBER CLEANING TOOL

He is like an electric toothbrush and he's battery operated so you don't have to worry about recharging him. He is life. I bought my first one on eBay and it was under £10, but I lent it to Mum and didn't get it back because she loved it so much too! It comes with several detachable heads and they're all good for different things. One is really good for tile grouting, one is really good for taps and another for the washing machine drawer. He gets into the hard-to-reach places or tricky gaps. I use Stewart mainly with The Pink Stuff or a paste-type cleaner.

SPONTEX MICROFIBRE KITCHEN CLOTHS

Awww, my Buddy (yellow) and Brian (blue). These come in packs of two for £3 and they're the dream team. You can soak them or put them in the washing machine again and again and they'll come up like new.

SPRAY BOTTLE

We all need spray bottles! I've got spray bottles filled with diluted Zofloras and diluted fabric conditioner, and I use them every day. I love labelling them up and deciding which one I fancy using each day. You can buy spray bottles from most places cheaply enough, and you will use them time and time again.

VACUUM STORAGE BAGS

Barbara Bags! These have revolutionised my wardrobe. I buy them in Poundland or Poundstretcher and the linen-scented ones are my favourites. In the summer I vacuum-bag my winter clothes and vice versa. I then store them under the bed. It keeps my wardrobe organised and keeps the clothes folded away neatly until the weather is right to bring them back out.

VILEDA 1-2 SPRAY MICROFIBRE FLAT SPRAY MOP

My lovely Vera. You fill her up with a diluted Zoflora mix or even your fave floor cleaner. Press the trigger to spray her and off you go! Don't ever let Vera go thirsty, no one deserves to be treated that way!

VILEDA TURBO MICROFIBRE MOP

My good old Trace wanted something named after her so this mop became Trace the Turbo mop. And boy, is she turbo charged (I'm talking about both Trace and the mop here). I find this mop so fun to use! Pop the mop head into the bucket for a good rinse and then press your foot down on the pedal to give her a good blow dry! Then she's ready to go. Your floors will shine bright like a diamond!

VILEDA WINDOWMATIC VACUUM

Our Victor! I take genuine pleasure in letting him work his magic on my windows and shower doors. No streaks, no annoying droplets left behind. He works a treat.

TOP TIP: I also use Victor to vacuum up spillages from Henry's water bowl.

BASKET HEAVEN

I love being organised so I do make sure everything has its own place in my home. I literally have baskets for absolutely everything, from tea towels to place mats to cleaning products and medication. As you've probably seen, I've even got them in my fridge to keep cheese and sauces in. All the best, Soph!

I love my belly baskets too, which keep my blankets organised and create a mini-feature in any room.

Now I do have my two 'mains': the famous shopping-style baskets with handles that I couldn't be without. They both sit in my kitchen Narnia. They were £3.99 each from Poundstretcher, but I cannot for the life of me get hold of them any more! I even messaged Poundstretcher and said my Hinchers really need these baskets, where are they? But no luck as yet. I'll keep trying! One is my daily basket and one is my weekly basket. They're perfect because it means I can carry them around the house by their little handles when I'm hinching, and just have the best time! The following baskets are my mains:

DAILY BASKET

————————

1001 Carpet Fresh Spray

o

Astonish Window and Glass Spray

o

Bloo Foam Aroma

o

Buff Tings Mop Slippers

o

Cif Power and Shine Wipes

o

Dave the Fluffy Duster

o

Febreze Fabric Freshener Spray

o

Flash Bathroom Spray

o

Gregory Rubber Gloves

o

Harpic Active Fresh Pine Toilet Cleaner

o

Hoover attachments

o

Mr Sheen Multi Surface Polish

o

Zoflora

o

WEEKLY BASKET

Astonish All Purpose Descaler

o

Astonish Mould and Mildew Spray

o

Astonish Specialist Hob and Cooktop
Cleaner and Sponge

o

Bicarbonate of soda

o

Carex handwash refill

o

Clothes lint brush

o

Elbow Grease

o

Flash Bathroom Liquid Cleaner 1L

o

Flash Floor Cleaner

o

Oven and hob scraper

o

Soda crystals

o

Stardrops Leather Clean and Feed

o

Toilet Duck Fresh Discs and Fresh Strips in Pine

o

Tumble dryer sheets

o

Viakal

o

White vinegar

o

Zoflora

o

LAUNDRY BASKET

Ace For Whites

o

Ariel Gel

o

Astonish Oxy Active Plus

o

Dettol Washing Machine Cleaner

o

Dr Beckmann In-Wash Stain Remover

Dylon Brilliant White Repair Sachets

o

Lenor Spring Awakening Fabric
Conditioner

o

Lenor Unstoppables Fresh In-Wash
Scent Boosters

o

Zoflora

o

SINK BASKET

Cif Cream Original with Micro Crystals

o

Cliff the Cif Stainless Steel Spray

o

Dishmatics

o

Fairy Platinum Washing-Up Liquid

o

Fairy Power Spray

o

SonicScrubber

o

Stardrops Pine and Astonish Germ
Clear Disinfectant Sprays

o

The Pink Stuff

o

Zoflora

o

BEFORE-BED BLAST

Dettol All In One Spray

o

Febreze Air Frosted Pine

o

Lenor Febreze Spring Awakening

o

And many, many more . . .

o

CLOTH BASKET

Buddy and Brian

o

Clarence the Polish Cloth

o

Kermit

o

Microfibre cloths

o

Minkehs

o

Minky scourers

o

Pinkehs

o

Scrub Daddy

o

AD HOC BASKET

Astonish Hob Cream Cleaner

o

Bicarbonate of soda

o

Dishwasher tablets

o

Soda crystals

o

Steam Microwave Cleaner

o

Toilet tablets

o

Tumble dryer sheets

o

Vamoosh Pet Hair Dissolver

o

MUSIC MOTIVATES
ME TO CLEAN

I find music so motivational to hinch to. I think it's the rhythm. I don't know about anyone else, but I love to mime along to songs, and I get right into it!

If I'm listening to a song and I've got a room to finish cleaning, the beat of that song will drive me on to give a little bit more. It's like being in the gym when you'll give it another five minutes on the treadmill if a banging track comes on.

I am the biggest Beyoncé fan going. I've been to every show of hers. I think she is amazing. Something about listening to her music makes me feel really strong. She's so inspirational. Put a Beyoncé track on for me and I'll be dancing around the room with Vera and singing into her handle as if it's a mic (don't judge).

Music makes people feel happy and if there's a song that brings back a good memory, it can instantly transport you to that time. There are so many amazing R&B songs that remind me of nights out with the girls or holidays with Jamie.

There are also certain songs that remind me of times in my life that were hard, but now I like listening to those songs because it makes me realise how far I've come. They make me feel good about myself rather than fearful of where I've been and the tough times. We've all been through hard times and we've all worked through it, and for me, facing up to it has taken the sting out of it.

Sometimes, when I feel a bit nervous and I feel like I'm going to start panicking, I'll put on a good song and it helps me more than anything. The combination of that and cleaning is such a win! They've pulled me through some of my hardest times.

Obviously no playlist is complete without the Minkeh song, Drake's 'In My Feelings', and here are my other fave tracks to hinch to.

MY ULTIMATE HINCHING PLAYLIST

---

o Aretha Franklin – 'Respect'

Everyone knows that this is my Cliff the Cif song. He was the first product I ever used on my stories so I've got a lot of respect for him. That is honestly why I chose this song.

o Ariana Grande – 'Breathin''

I was steaming the floors and I needed a word that rhymed with steaming and this popped up. Result.

- Barry White – 'Can't Get Enough Of Your Love, Babe'

  My mum and I love a bit of Barry White. His voice is so soothing.

- Beyoncé – 'Flawless'

  Beyoncé is my absolute idol. Whenever I listen to her I feel like this really strong woman. It's embarrassing but it's true.

- Big Brovaz – 'Baby Boy'

  Me and my girls always used to play this when we went in my friend's mum's car. She had a convertible so it always takes me back to that time.

- Brandy & Monica – 'The Boy Is Mine'

  I literally chose this song because 'mine' rhymes with 'pine', so I play this when I'm using Paul the Pine.

- Bruno Mars – '24K Magic'

I think Bruno Mars is one of the best dancers on the planet. I wouldn't say I'm quite as good when I'm trying to copy his moves but I love the beat of this song.

○ The Countdown Kids – 'Baby Shark'

My life was made when this song came out and worked so perfectly with Sharon the Shark. It's a song I love to hate!

○ Destiny's Child – 'Survivor'

We're all basically trying to survive in this crazy world we live in and there's so much passion in this song.

○ Drake – 'In My Feelings'

A follower of mine, @thethompsonhome, wrote some lyrics out to this song and said it reminded her of me, so it became synonymous with my account. It's also just a bloody great song.

○ Drake – 'Started From The Bottom'

This first came about when I got sent my Mrs Hinch Fairy bottle, because I was thinking to myself, 'What song says, "Look where I am now"?' Then a Hincher messaged me and said, 'You started from the bottom, Mrs Hinch.' So I changed the lyrics to 'I started from the bottom and now we're hinched'. Now I play it every time I get a personalised item.

○ Elton John – 'Can You Feel The Love Tonight'

I used this when I did my Harry Potter understairs Hinch reveal. I do feel the love when I've hinched something, and it's such a dramatic song so it works perfectly.

○ Elvis Presley – 'All Shook Up'

I was cleaning the floor with Vera one day and I thought, 'I've got such a wide range of ages amongst my Hinchers.' I wanted to include songs for every age group, and who doesn't love Elvis?

○ Fabolous ft Ashanti – 'So Into You'

Everyone my age loves this song. When I put this on my stories more people message me about this song than any other one.

○ Freya Ridings – 'Lost Without You'

'You' rhymes with Bloo so it became the Bloo Foam Aroma song. I first heard it on *Love Island* and loved it.

○ Karen Harding – 'Say Something'

When Mr Hinch did his Instagram takeover he put down on his list of things to do 'spray something', and that morphed into 'say something'. I love Karen Harding.

○ K-Ci & JoJo – 'Tell Me It's Real'

This was Mr Hinch's idea. I wanted a song to hinch to and he suggested this. Genius.

○ Lil' Romeo – 'My Cinderella'

This is another teenage song
from back in the day. It's such a tune.

○ Luther Vandross – 'Never Too Much'

No one is ever going to turn Luther
off. Everyone loves him so he often
features on my stories.

○ Mario – 'Let Me Love You'

This song reminds me of when I was
about fourteen. I used to play it
before I went out.

○ Matoma & Becky Hill – 'False Alarm'

When you put this song on you are
ready to go out. The start of it really
lifts me so it makes me either want
to go out with my friends, or start
hinching to high hell.

○ Michael Jackson – 'This Is It'

The words to this song are
unbelievable. I feel like I'm bringing
everyone together when I play

Michael Jackson's songs because we all know them.

o Ne-Yo – 'Sexy Love'

Ne-Yo is such an amazing dancer and I love trying to pull off some of his moves when I'm having a sesh with Vera.

o Pretty Ricky – 'On The Hotline'

I used this song when I cleaned my worktops once because Pinkeh rhymed with Ricky. Then I listened to it and I thought, 'I forgot how much I love this tune.'

o Rudimental ft Ella Eyre – 'Waiting All Night'

It's the video for this song that gets me. It's really inspirational. If you haven't watched it, please do. The chorus is so strong and upbeat it gets me motivated.

o Tyga – 'Taste'

This song was one of the new releases on iTunes so I gave it a whirl, and once I listened to it I realised it's got a great beat for when you're cleaning your bathroom with Minkeh.

○ Usher – 'Trading Places'

This is by far the sexiest song on the planet. Me and Natalie, who is like my music twin, will play this on repeat when we're in the car together.

○ Usher – 'U Got It Bad'

I think Usher's voice is unbelievable and he's ridiculously handsome.

○ Usher – 'U Remind Me'

Usher is all about the memories for me and this song takes me right back to my teens.

○ Wham – 'Wake Me Up Before You Go-Go'

I play this in the morning to get me up and get me in the mood for the day.

○ Whitney Houston – 'Greatest Love Of All'

Whitney is Whitney. She's so incredible. I often use Whitney's songs when I'm doing reveals, like when I rejig Narnia, and also when I'm putting Henry to bed.

○ Whitney Houston – 'One Moment In Time'

More Whitney. It's another dramatic reveal song. I wanted a song that has the word 'moment' in it, and this is such a classic.

DIARY

○ What are your top sayings?

....

....

....

○ What are your favourite hinch haul shops?

....

....

....

○ What's on your 'to buy' list?

....

....

....

○ What's the best barg you've ever picked up?

....

....

....

○ Have you got any funny names for your cloths?

....

....

....

○ What makes your laundry smell amazing?

....

....

....

○ What one thing in your house could you never get rid of?

....

....

....

○ What are your top five songs to hinch to?

1) ....

2) ....

3) ....

4) ....

5) ....

PART THREE
A Bit About Me

CHAPTER FIVE

I'VE ALWAYS BEEN A HOMEBODY

know my Instagram account is mainly about cleaning, but I'm being asked more and more about my personal life, like how I met Jamie and who my closest friends are, as well as how I manage my worry and anxiety, so this is the perfect place for me to tell you a bit more about me, about Sophie.

HERE WE GO . . .

I was born in Basildon Hospital. My mum has still got the tiny T-shirt she brought me home in that says, 'I was born in Basildon Hospital.' I'm like, 'Mum, really?'

We moved about a bit when I was younger but then once we settled in our little village in 1994, that was it. I've lived here ever since and it's home.

I was a very needy child, stuck to my mum 24/7. She couldn't even find a nursery I would settle in! But three nurseries later and I was finally content! As I was growing up, ironically, my room was a mess. My mum was always telling me to clear up after myself and I'd roll my eyes thinking, 'Oh, leave me alone.'

I'd leave things lying around and Mum would say, 'Does that live there?' and I'd be like, 'Nooooo, I suppose not.' I used to think it was so ridiculous that she worried about things being messy and I'm sure I used to think a cleaning fairy walked around behind me all the time clearing up (well, she did – she was called my mum, bless her!).

They do say you turn into your mum as you get older (which I would actually love), and I do the same thing to Jamie now as she did to me. Last summer I found myself asking him, 'Do your flip-flops live outside the shoe cupboard? Are they going to walk themselves into there? No.' Well then!

I was so messy growing up that I would step out of my

pyjamas and leave them on the floor where they fell. I wasn't a naughty child, but I was haphazard, clumsy, and I didn't know the value of things in the home back then. I remember once putting my brand-new roller skates on. I was literally buzzing on life. I leant up against the wall for a rest, my feet wheeled out from underneath me and I landed on my hand and fractured my wrist! Two operations and a few pins later and my wrist was on the mend! Only I could break my wrist standing stationary!

I idolise my mum and dad, Freda and Alan. My dad is like a big bear and he probably looks quite intimidating to other people, but he's far from it. If he watches something remotely emotional on the TV, I guarantee you he'll be the one crying. My mum is the toughest cookie you'll ever meet and I've probably only seen her cry twice in twenty-eight years. She lost her dad and her older brother when she was in her teen-age years, so she took on the mother role in her household from a young age. Her younger brothers and sister still look up to her now for support. She's a rock to so many of us, and the strongest woman I know. I am more like my dad in that I'm very sensitive and I love my food, but things like wanting my home to feel homely and organised and looking after people are definitely things I get from my mum.

They say opposites attract and I have to agree! My mum and her family are from London's East End and my dad and his family are from Durham in the North-East, so some may say I've got a bit of a whacky mix.

My mum works in the florist in our village and has done for over eighteen years, and my dad is a Project Director for a large construction company. He has a very stressful job so he was often away working during the week when I was growing up, and then he'd be home at the weekends. My parents met when my mum was working behind a bar and my dad went in for a drink. He took her out for a Chinese and the rest is history, I guess. Now don't get me wrong, they squabble, they bicker, and they've had their fair share of arguments (haven't we all), but more than thirty years later they are still together and I know deep down they couldn't live without each other!

Mum inspired me house-wise when I was growing up. She enjoys redecorating and reorganising, and from the age of eleven I used to look in all the interior catalogues and magazines with her and circle the things we would love in the house. She'd say, 'I'm gonna get that lamp, Soph,' and I'd say, 'Those cushions would go really well with it.' We'd write down the catalogue numbers and it was like we were redecorating together.

When I was about fourteen Mum and Dad told me they were going to redecorate my bedroom because it was a bit too young for me. I had the Love Hearts sweets wallpaper at the time, so I have to agree! You know when you go from being a kid to a teenager all of a sudden and your tastes completely change? It was like that, and I was so excited. My dad said to me, 'We're going to take you out and whatever wallpaper you choose, you can have.' I was like, 'YES!'

I liked really dark colours at the time. We went into Laura Ashley in Billericay and I went for a dark plum wallpaper with a lighter plum swirl through it.

My room wasn't that big so my mum said it would look far too dark.

Dad convinced her it could work okay if we got lighter furniture for my room, but oh no, I also had my heart set on dark oak furniture.

Bless them, my parents agreed to let me have my dark bedroom and I have to say, once the room was decorated, even my mum said it looked amazing. My dad bought me the thickest cream pile carpet going. When I walked on it you could still see the footprints. It was like a blanket of snow. I was so obsessed with the whole thing.

It's funny because my older sister Samantha is the total opposite to me. She also had her bedroom redecorated at the same time but she wasn't fussed at all. She wouldn't have minded if it had bare walls with just a bed in the middle of the room as long as she could sleep! She loved her sleep and loved going out with her friends! I remember creeping into her room in the mornings to get the hairdryer, and if I woke her up . . . mate! I would run for my life!

Sam's home, which she shares with her husband, is beautifully clean and tidy. She has two dogs (Henry's fur cousins, he loves them so much) and a daughter, my niece Abi, who also loves to keep her room looking pretty! She's ten and she doesn't care about having the latest pair of trainers or phone, but she's very into her bedroom. When she comes to my house she says, 'Auntie Sophie, I'm going to have a house like yours one day. Will you help me decorate it?'

She had her bedroom redecorated recently and she asked for grey, white and silver décor like my house. It's so cute. Last Christmas I didn't get her games like I usually do, I got her lovely things to go in her bedroom. I even got her a reed diffuser and a lamp the same as mine, and a little fake tea light so she could put it in her lantern. It looks like a mini version of my place and she absolutely loves it and it makes her so happy. She's such a caring, sensitive and intelligent little girl and I'm just so proud of her!

My newly decorated bedroom was also my absolute pride and joy. When I was about fifteen I started going out more and experimenting with drinking with my friends, as you do. One night I came home after a night out and I'd had a bit too much alcohol (I'm sure it was that Lambrini you could buy for £1.99 a bottle, oh dear). I remember sitting on the edge of my bed, my head spinning, and thinking, 'I feel seriously sick. This is so grim.' Then I threw up all over my hair. I flung my head back and sick went all over my new wallpaper and covered my carpet. The wallpaper was marked and the carpet looked terrible, and no matter what I did to it I could not get the marks out of the wallpaper.

I remember crying to my parents and being so sorry. I was sobbing, 'I can't believe I've ruined my room!' So my first ever Mrs Hinch room, guys, was beautiful for a little while, and then I totally ruined it. It was so upsetting. My parents were good about it, considering, but they must have been fuming, mate.

As my Hinchers know, the silver plush rug in my living room is my absolute pride and joy. If anyone did to my rug what I did to my bedroom carpet I would be devastated. You really do live and learn.

When I left school I went to sixth form to study psychology, geography and media studies. I got my first-ever job as a childcare assistant at an after-school club. When I was growing up I wanted to be a primary school teacher, so I really enjoyed working with all the kids. I worked there three afternoons a week. Mum would drop me off after college and it was such a great focus for me. That time reading to the kids gave me some relief from all the panicky thoughts I had, which started when I was young.

It's hard to explain because I am confident in some ways, and I love meeting new people and having a good chat! So I would describe it as a form of anxiety, but it's more on the paranoia/nervous side. Anyway, whatever I did, I could never seem to get over it.

I've always been a worrier. At school I would really envy the girls who were so laid-back, and there was me, worrying about whether I'd got my PE kit or if I was going to make the next class on time. I look back now and they were such small things, but they consumed me.

I'd get home from school and I'd analyse my day. I'd think back over everything I'd said in case I had offended anyone.

I'd think about anything I could potentially have done wrong. No one else caused it, it was all inside my head. I would worry about things that hadn't even happened.

Sometimes I'd only be back home for five minutes and my paranoia would kick in, so I'd have to phone one of my school friends just to make sure they were still talking to me. I didn't have a mobile phone so if I called their landline and it was engaged, I would convince myself they were probably on the phone to another friend discussing something I'd done wrong. That's how bad it was.

I suffered terribly with a few girls when I first started secondary school (I'm sure we all go through it), to the point where I was so nervous about going in each morning that my stomach was in knots and I couldn't eat. The weight just fell off so fast! I do wonder if some of my worrying stems from that. But the bottom line is, I'm also a really sensitive person so I believe I was just destined to be a worrier.

I was around twelve when it started and the worst of it lasted around eight months. I can put my hand on my heart even to this day and say that nothing else has ever compared to the anxiety I felt when that was going on. Even now, I am so relieved that I'm not going through any of that any more, and when I see children walking to school I just pray they don't feel that way or ever have to go through anything like that.

The thing about school is that you have to go, there's no choice! You can't run away from the situation. It got to the point where my mum met with the teachers to try and find a way to stop it, but nothing helped.

One day my mum dropped me off at the school gates. It was raining and two girls shut the doors and held them tight so I had to stand outside in the rain. I got completely drenched! I was trying to find another way to get into the building because I was going to be late for class and I was in a serious flap.

But it turned out my mum hadn't gone home that day. She decided, for whatever reason, to stay parked up in her car outside the school. Mother's instinct, I guess! She got out of the car, came over and said, 'Come on, Soph, get in the car, you're not going to school today.' I broke down in tears just hearing her voice. I've never needed my mum so much in my life! She took me home and we got so snug indoors and watched films all day. I remember it so well because it was a Friday, and it was the best feeling ever knowing I had three whole days with my mum until I had to go back and face school again.

I had a TV in my room at the time, and every morning before I went to school I'd pause it on a certain part of a film I was watching, which was quite often *The Borrowers* (mine and my mum's favourite film). I would tell myself all I had to do was get through the day and the film would be waiting for me. When I got back from school and the film was still paused in the same place it would make me feel like 'I did it'. I'd press play and I felt like I could pretend the last six hours hadn't happened, and that life was okay.

My mum and I became closer than ever during this time, and I remember thinking, 'I can't wait to be a grown-up lady at home all the time.' I honestly think that's why I love being at home so much now, because, to me, it feels like the safest place.

There was nothing I cherished more than staying in on a Friday night with my mum and dad and ordering a Chinese takeaway. Mum and I would then go through the TV magazine and circle everything we wanted to watch that night (there was no Sky Plus back then), and that was my idea of a perfect evening.

Even though that time was awful, the best thing ever came out of it! I met the group of girls, aka The Kids, who are still my best friends to this day. One day I was eating my lunch alone on the stairs near the art rooms when Tanya walked past. She said to me, 'What *are* you doing eating on the stairs?' (How embarrassing.)

We started chatting. We remembered each other from primary school, and she invited me round to her house after school. After that, I ended up going there after school most days. We discovered that we both loved singing on the karaoke machine and playing shops (we were twelve at the time and both knew we were a bit old for that, so we didn't tell anyone, but for Christmas our mums bought us a till and mate, it was life!) and from there this bond formed instantly.

After that Tanya and I formed a friendship group with the rest of 'the kids'. We've been a solid group of five ever since. I'll be forever grateful to these girls because, to this day they don't know it, but they got me through the hardest time in my life.

They didn't expect anything in return; they were just there for me. We're a package deal and they were all my bridesmaids when Mr Hinch and I tied the knot. So to my kids . . . I thank you and I love you.

The kids will always be my best friends and we'll always have each other's backs. We text each other every day in our group chat and we do everything together, whether it's going out for our birthdays or having a junk-food night in.

I do know one thing for certain though; if I'm ever really successful, I am taking the five of us away somewhere really nice for a proper girls' holiday! Kids on Tour.

The girls know I don't really drink because I really went off the taste of it for some reason, plus I find that I get really panicky when I've got a hangover, aka Beer Fear. It heightens the anxiety and I end up spending the whole of the next day worrying about what I've said and done.

The only thing I'll drink every now and again is (wait for it) a WKD Blue. It's so embarrassing because it's bright blue so everyone knows exactly what you're drinking, but it's the only alcoholic drink I can stomach the taste of. It's like drinking sweets but, let's be honest, it's frowned upon when anyone of my age drinks it! But my best friends understand me so well and they're the best kids I could ever ask for.

The most amazing thing ever happened when this young girl sent me a DM. She told me that she was being bullied at school and that my Instagram stories made her laugh and would take her mind off things. She messaged me again and said that she really didn't want to go to school the following day. I told her that I would be on my phone checking my messages from her all day whilst she was at school and she could message me at any time and I would reply! I didn't put my phone down that day.

The following day she messaged me and said: 'Mrs Hinch, I did it, I got through the day, and when I got home my mum had bought me the floor wipes that were on your story so I can hinch the bathroom floor and I can't wait to show you the before and after pic.'

It absolutely melted my heart. I shared her post on my story and she couldn't believe it, bless her! To be able to help someone who is going through a bad time meant so much to me. So you know who you are, my Hincher! I told you everything would be okay, and now look, you not only made my story, but now you've also made my book!

In a lot of ways what happened to me during that really difficult time changed my life for the better. I have no resentment towards anyone whatsoever. So, wherever you are, girls, I hope things are good for you. And from my heart, I wish you all the best.

I have amazing friends and I know how lucky I am, but my sister Sam is also my absolute rock, and her, me and our mum are like The Three Musketeers.

A Bit About My Kids

TANYA

Tanya comes out with some cracking comments. Her blonde one-liners are just hilarious. She was the first one I clung on to when I was going through a hard time at school, and she saved me, really. Our mums are close friends, we share a love for our homes and I'm so proud of her.

NATALIE

Natalie is my music twin. We both love R&B, a good dance and making sure our selfie game is strong. Nat has a serious resting bitch face and says it how it is, but you will not find anyone more caring than her. She will message me most days just asking if I'm okay, and she will have your back no matter what! She would defend me to the end of the earth!

LEANNE

Our mummy of the group. She'll organise the taxis, make sure we've got money and our phones, but most importantly she'll always make sure we are safe and together. I've known Leanne since I was five and first moved to the village. She's such a strong person who has had the toughest time the past year and I can honestly say she is one of the bravest, strongest women I know.

COLLETTE

By far the most forgetful kid in the group! But she's the most selfless person I know. She will always put other people first and will always check up on me to make sure my anxiety is under control. I always feel calmer when I'm around Collette because I know she understands me, and she knows what I'm thinking without me telling her. If that's not a best friend then I don't know what is.

My Other BFFs

TRACE

A lot of you have seen and experienced my Trace on my stories. The Ikea story is a particular classic. You know when you have that one friend that you argue with like a sister most days but couldn't live without? That's Trace to me! She will always make me laugh and tells me how it is. We are just as bonkers as each other but I wouldn't have her any other way. My Trace always x

GEORGIA AND FAITH

My little duo! They have supported me so much. We're really close and we're always there for each other – we may not speak every day but I just know when I need them they are there for me. They were also my bridesmaids. People were shocked at how many bridesmaids I had, but I couldn't and wouldn't leave any of my girls out.

And there's more!

After I left sixth form, I got a telesales job in Chelmsford selling advertising to tradesmen over the phone, and believe it or not, I smashed it. I really enjoyed it, and I think that was because I was behind the phone and I could hide, in a way. A little like my Instagram stories; no one can judge you on your appearance and I love that!

I left that post when I got a job working in London when I was twenty-three, and that's when I met Jamie. He was working as a team leader and he had to train me on some parts of the job. I wasn't really listening to what he was saying because I was thinking, 'You're nice. But God, you talk too much!' (He still does, to be fair. Haha!)

I'd never experienced the working life in London and everyone was going out drinking together every single night, including me in the end! Up until that point I'd never even been on a train or tube on my own because I was a 'village girl', so it came as a shock. I felt like a fish out of water, but I was really spreading my wings. It was scary at first, but it allowed me to grow.

I'd go out with work colleagues and then catch the last train home, get up the following morning and do it all again. If you told me I had to do that again now I'd probably run a mile because I like being in front of the TV in my pyjamas with my blanket, but I had such a great time whilst the fun lasted.

I'll be honest, London did intimidate me a bit at first, but I was having so much fun I didn't even have the time to worry or deep-think as much. I remember looking around the office and everyone was so well dressed that I felt a bit dated and behind the times. Also it didn't help that my eyebrows were basically higher than Mount Everest, mate. They were literally at the top of my head. When I look back I can't believe I walked into the office with them like that. They were *not* on fleek, guys.

All the girls in the office were so gorgeous, their hair, nails, lashes and clothes were beautiful! It was very much about what you had and what you wore (that's London, though), which was all very alien to me. I didn't have lots of money and I still used to shop at the local village boutique. But they were such lovely girls to me and I became really friendly with them. I'm still in touch with a lot of them now. You know who you are, girls! (All the best!)

Jamie and I used to spend a lot of time chatting together and he would make me laugh every day. After a while I knew I was starting to like him. But I was shy and, having struggled with my weight, my confidence was low. I still felt big, which brings me neatly on to the next thing I want to talk about.

CHAPTER SIX

HIGHS, LOWS
AND BECOMING
MRS HINCH

Started from the bottom now we're Hinched!

When I was twenty-one, and thought I knew everything, I had a gastric band fitted and I've lost just over eight stone since 2011.

The first thing I want to say is that I know gastric bands work amazingly for some people who are seriously overweight, but my personal experience was an absolute nightmare, and I'm still dealing with the repercussions to this day. It's caused me nothing but complications and it put my life at risk, which we'll come on to.

I was young and naïve and I took out a bank loan of £6,000 to get it done privately, without telling my family or friends. I made a rash decision that a big part of me regrets.

I've always felt so ashamed about my gastric band. When I told my mum I was going to talk about it in the book she said to me, 'Soph, you haven't committed a crime or hurt anyone but yourself,' and she's right. But I would hate for anyone to read this and think I am advocating weight loss surgery in any way, because I am in fact doing the exact opposite.

I think I was in denial about my size for a long time, and then one day I went to get on a ride at Southend-on-Sea Adventure Island and I couldn't fit in the seat. The safety bar just wouldn't stay shut. Having to get off that ride was the most humiliating feeling I've ever had and I could just feel eyes staring at me. After that, I felt more uncomfortable than ever. People look at you differently when you're bigger. I don't care what anyone says, there are certain people that do and it doesn't go unnoticed. In hindsight, I know that I should never have let that affect me, but unfortunately it did.

I'm not expecting people to get the violin out here, but when people message me now on Instagram and say, 'You don't understand what it's like being big, Mrs Hinch,' I'm thinking to myself, 'Trust me, I do. I've been there. I've been almost double the size I am now.' People are so complimentary to me now, but I struggle with the compliments because inside I am the same person I always have been. My insecurities, believe it or not, are still the same, if not worse.

At that age I just wanted to be smaller and look like everyone else when they were out in their dresses and high-heeled shoes. It was as simple as that. I was naïve and I did something that I will always regret. If I could go back in time I definitely wouldn't do it again.

I wish I'd been older, I wish I hadn't done it in secret and I wish I'd known about the health risks! And most of all, I wish I hadn't felt so despairing in the first place that I felt the need to put my body through that.

The thing about life is that what gets you through the dark times is hope. You hope things will get better, and you hope making a change will shift things. Even when you're at rock bottom there's always that bit of you that has to keep believing you can turn your life around. I was very overweight and very unhappy with my appearance, and no matter what crazy quick-fix diet I tried the weight would always pile back on.

I know people have much bigger issues in their lives, but the anxiety around my size was relentless for me. I was battling with it every single day and it was making me so low.

I always felt so much bigger than everyone else. I'm five foot ten so I am above average height for a girl. My mum would always say, 'Soph, supermodels are tall, tall is beautiful,' and as much as I wanted to feel this way, I didn't. I felt like I was in the way and took up too much space in a room. As a teen I was taller than all the boys my age, which didn't help. I felt so awkward and thought no one would ever fancy me.

So one day, in desperation, I typed 'best way to lose weight' into Google and gastric bands came straight up. It seemed like the easiest way for me to be able to look like the other girls and be able to wear pretty little dresses and feel good. Little did I know.

I phoned this clinic that was offering gastric bands and within two weeks I'd taken out a loan and I was having it fitted. Even up until recently some of my friends didn't know because I didn't want to admit to people what I'd done to myself, but now I have so much support around me that I'm facing up to it and realising I haven't hurt anyone, so why do I feel ashamed?

IT HAD TO HAPPEN TO ME

In 2013 my band slipped, which is rare but can happen occasionally, and it ended up wedged in my oesophagus. My mum had to take me to A&E because I was in agony and that's when I had to admit to her what I'd done.

I had to have an emergency operation to move the band back to my stomach, but it was so dangerous, and I couldn't believe it had happened to me. I was so scared. I said, 'What have I done, Mum?'

It was a slow road to recovery but I got through it. My band was back in the right place but it was 'unclipped' so it wasn't restricting my food intake. I didn't care at the time. I was just so relieved that my stomach and oesophagus were still in one piece!

I then had an operation in 2016 that ended in disaster. After such a big weight loss, I was very lucky that my skin seemed to ping back into shape really well. I assume, because I was so young, the elasticity was still there! I hadn't been left with any loose skin, apart from on my arms, which became a serious issue in the end.

The rest of my body was fine, but for some reason my arms really suffered and as a result they looked out of proportion. If I bought a size 10 or 12 top or jacket in a shop it would fit me everywhere else, but not the arms. I was smaller, but I still couldn't buy clothes in the size that I actually was.

I kept getting problems with the excess skin. It was getting inflamed and blistering. It was painful.

I went to see my doctor to ask for some cream for an infection in my armpit and he said to me, 'This isn't a cosmetic issue, it's a medical issue. We need to remove the excess skin from your arms or you're going to have problems for the rest of your life.' As a result, I was referred for more surgery to have the surplus skin removed.

The surgery seemed to go well and the hospital staff were amazing, but unfortunately, when I returned to the hospital for a post-op check, the surgeon told me I had an internal infection in my left arm! At first I thought I had the flu because I had a temperature, but then as the days went on both arms blew up almost three times in size and they had to drain them urgently and blast me with IV antibiotics. I ended up staying in hospital for two weeks and I genuinely thought I was going to lose my left arm at one point. Thankfully they managed to find a particular antibiotic that worked and killed the infection, but it was touch and go for a while.

I had to sit up in bed with my arms hooked through these giant foam hoops so they could drain. I even had to sleep like that, which was a challenge. Everyone who came on to the ward must have thought I was really overly friendly because it looked like I was waving constantly at anyone that walked by. But what did make me laugh was Collette strolling into the ward to visit me bearing gifts, one of which was a colouring book and pens! Well cheers, kid! I'll have fun just staring at that! It cracked us up for days!

Those two weeks made me realise that I am who I am and I can't put my body through any more risks. When my mum came to visit me, she looked at me and all she said was, 'Why are you doing this to yourself, Soph?' I started crying and replied, 'I'm sorry, Mum, I really am.'

Of course I had to rest my arms, so when I finally got back home there was no hinching for me, and that was hard. I went through such a difficult time mentally, and I knew that cleaning would help me to reset and feel calmer, but I had to allow my arms to heal.

I wasn't able to hoover or karate chop my cushions so Jamie had to do all the cleaning for me. And anyone who's seen my video of Jamie trying to hinch knows he's not the most productive Hincher out there, bless him, but he did amazingly well. In fact, when he did his Mr Hinch takeover on my story, two of the to-do tasks were 'make a drink' and 'have dessert'. I don't think he's what you'd call a natural, but I love him for that.

I'm so grateful to everyone at the hospital that helped me, and my arms are now what are considered to be a good size for my frame, so I can buy coats and tops that fit every bit of me. I use a Powerspin device regularly to exercise my arms now to make sure I keep the blood flowing well, and I keep my eye on them to make sure they're not getting inflamed again.

Of course I've got scars, but they're a part of me. I thought I would have to cover my arms up for the rest of my life, but I was able to wear my dream strapless dress with a sweetheart neckline on my wedding day, which was everything.

If I get the odd troll criticising me for a decision I made when I was young and scared, I can't control that and I have to try and let it go. I am not perfect and I've made mistakes. I want to be open about it and say once again, I understand that gastric bands can save some people's lives but, personally, I am not promoting them. I could have lost so much as a result of mine. It's affected my long-term health and nothing is worth that.

I still can't get my head around the fact that I did that to myself. It's a major operation and I put myself through so much. My band is still on my stomach but it's completely deflated so it's no longer working as such. I would one day like to have the band removed but, because I'm currently on blood thinners, doctors have advised against it for now.

It wasn't comfortable feeling so full after eating such a small amount of food, but now I can go out for dinner with Jamie and relax and enjoy myself. I'm eating relatively well and taking care of myself and that's a huge change for me. Unfortunately I don't like fruit but I love vegetables so they're my main source of nutrients, but as my followers know, I do eat some rubbish at times and I love a bit of chocolate. But after years of not being able to eat much I'm treating myself, and if I put on some weight, who cares? I'm still here to tell the tale and even write the book.

I'm now learning to embrace my height and be happy with who I am. I've always worried that people would meet me for the first time and be disappointed. The book tour will be a big step for me, but I know my Hinchers will understand, and I can't wait to meet you all!

I had to have some time off work due to the complications of my band slipping. Jamie noticed I wasn't in the office, so he used to check in a lot to make sure that I was okay. He really is the friendliest person ever, so I didn't know if he liked me or was just being a concerned mate.

As the months went on we both realised it was more than 'just friends'. We would always be the last two left at the end of the nights out with everyone after work, just sitting chatting about anything and everything. One afternoon he sent me an email to ask if I fancied some dinner after work. I'll be honest, I wanted to scream I was so excited, but I knew he was looking over at me from his desk so I really tried to read the email but still play it cool! So I just kept a straight face, read the email and replied, 'Yeah, sounds good, I'm starving!' Truth is, I wanted to scream 'YES' across the office!

I was watching the clock on my computer counting down to 5 o'clock! I had serious butterflies and I felt nervous! Even though we had all been out together as a work team many times, I had never been with him completely on my own, one on one, and I had certainly never sat down and eaten a meal with him. I popped to the Ladies just before 5, topped up my make-up, brushed my hair, blasted myself in perfume and made sure I looked half presentable. I walked outside the office and there he was waiting for me, and he said, 'Come on then, let's go!'

We walked the streets of London for a while. I remember feeling so proud and safe walking around with him. Oxford Street really is beautiful so it was quite romantic and London fascinated me because it was all still so new to me! Finally we stopped in a road that had a number of restaurants and he said, 'Take your pick!' But the only one I recognised was PizzaExpress, I couldn't even pronounce the others!

So I said, 'Let's go to PizzaExpress!'

'Really?' he said.

'Yes, I love it in there! Come on!'

So that's where we ended up! That was our first date. I remember Jamie ordered a pizza and I ordered the Caesar salad! Why I did that I don't know, I don't even like salad much! We've been back there many times since then and it always makes us laugh now. We can't order in PizzaExpress without him jokingly saying, 'Salad, babe?' I'm like, 'Nah, mate! Pizza all the way.'

The meal was perfect, I loved it, we laughed so much! At the end of the night he walked me back to Oxford Circus station and I went home. I don't even remember the journey because I was just buzzing and staring at my phone, waiting for him to text me saying something, anything! I just needed to know he had a good time too.

I was living back with my parents at the time and I got home extremely late that night so I crept in like a teenager, making sure I didn't wake them up. I crawled into bed and then my phone started flashing. It wasn't a text message, he was ringing me! I jumped out of bed, pacing around my bedroom, looking at my phone thinking, 'How do I answer this call?' I even practised saying hello three times – Hey, Hello, Hi! I froze! Then I answered.

'All right.' (I mean who even answers their phone like that?) I cringed immediately but couldn't exactly hang up!

'Hi, Soph, I checked your train times and just wanted to make sure you got home okay.'

'Er yeah, I'm home, just lying in bed watching a film now.'

'Ahh nice, what film?'

There was no film on. I lied. So I had to say the first film that came into my head! 'Casper.'

His reply: 'As in *Casper the Friendly Ghost*?'

'Yeah, do you like it?'

'I did when I was a kid.'

Great! I remember the face I was pulling to myself! Soph, you absolute idiot. Anyway, at the end of the call he thanked me for one of the best nights he'd ever had, and I just remember feeling my cheeks burning. I blushed and said 'Ditto!' The call ended with a 'Goodnight and see you at work tomorrow!' After we hung up I immediately walked over to my wardrobe, planning my outfit for work the next day. I just wanted to try and look nice for him. Anyway, as the weeks went on we had more and more dates, even meeting up at the weekends, and I felt so happy. He even took me to Cadbury World! Heaven.

Then one day after work we were walking to the pub with our sales director to meet up with the rest of the office for billing day drinks and he just came out with it.

'Are you two together, then?'

I literally wanted the ground to swallow me whole!

Jamie replied, 'Yep, we are, well, I hope we are.'

I said yes quicker than I've ever said yes in my life and that was it! I felt like I was floating to the pub after that! When we arrived in the pub a few people were looking over at us, and a few people asked us if we were together and I could hear some little whispers going on, then Jamie just stood up in front of everyone and said, 'Yes, we are together and I love her.'

Well, I didn't know what to say. I couldn't believe it. But I'm sure my smile said it all!

WHAT IS THIS ZOFLORA STUFF?

After we'd been together for around nine months Jamie and I moved in together and rented a small flat in Essex. That's when my love of cleaning really started.

Working in London and doing the whole after-work socialising and living the hundred-miles-an-hour lifestyle was great and I'm so glad I experienced it, but after three years I was ready to take a step back. I wanted to be at home more, I wanted to nest indoors and I was desperate for a dog, and it wasn't fair to have one if we were both out at work all day.

I had this real desire to become a hairdresser so Jamie said to me, 'Take a year out, go to evening college and study hairdressing.' So that's what I did. I went from being at work all day surrounded by other people to being at home in our little flat. I'll admit at first I did feel a little lonely, as our flat was a good forty-five-minute drive from my parents and my sister.

My deep-thinking and worrying really peaked around this time. That's when it was at its worst and the hardest to deal with, especially without seeing anyone but Jamie from one day to the next. I don't know what caused it to spike then, but it used to come over me in waves and the panic would be overwhelming. My chest would feel like it was on fire and I knew I had to find an outlet for those feelings.

Being in a block of flats meant our home always had a really strong smell of other people's cooking. I tried to get rid of it by using air fresheners but it lingered. Then one day my mum came round with this little bottle of something called Zoflora.

The bottle was half full and she told me to dilute it and spray it around, and assured me it would be the only thing I would be able to smell. I won't lie, I was a bit sceptical so I bunged it in the cupboard under my sink and forgot about it.

One day the food smell was really strong so I thought, 'I've got nothing to lose.' I got the little bottle out and mixed a capful with some water. I cleaned the floors with it, sprayed it everywhere, and when Jamie walked in he said to me, 'What's that smell? It's amazing.' He was right, and I was officially hooked on Zoflora.

I soon discovered there were other scents and I was off. Before I knew it, the cupboard under the sink was full of different-scented Zofloras. I was in heaven.

One day I decided to tidy up my growing collection and I thought about the medical basket my mum had when I was growing up. Lots of people have medical boxes but she always had a basket, and if ever we needed painkillers or plasters we knew where to go. I bought a little green plastic basket for my Zofloras. Then I bought another one for my medical stuff and that's how my basket collection kicked off too. Before I knew it, I was buying baskets for baskets.

I found that cleaning made me feel good. Who knew? That thing I always thought of as boring and a chore started to become really enjoyable, and the more products I discovered, the more I loved it.

Whenever I felt like my head was spiralling out of control I would grab a mop or a hoover and get stuck in. When you're focusing so much on what you're doing, you somehow stop focusing on the things that are making you feel uneasy. That was a life-changing discovery for me, in so many ways.

HERE COMES THE BRIDE

Jamie and I got married in August 2018 and my wedding day was genuinely the best day of my life.

I went to Brighton with my girls for my hen do a couple of weeks beforehand and it was such a brilliant way to say good-bye to my single years.

It was Pride weekend, so you can imagine what the atmosphere was like. We went to see the Dream Boys and had drinks and ate nice food. What could be better? I had the best hen and the best group of girls around me and I wish I could do it all again.

We had our wedding at Gosfield Hall in Essex and it was perfect. I spent a year planning it and worrying about it and making sure everyone had a good time. Of course, on the day my anxiety kicked in. I was worried that I would let people down because of what I looked like when I walked down the aisle, or Jamie wouldn't turn up. They were crazy emotions, but it all went perfectly and I still can't quite believe how brilliant it was. I wanted a traditional fairy-tale wedding and I got it.

Obviously my dress was a big part of it. I love all the elegant, sexy fitted numbers you can get, but I wanted that big Cinderella moment where people have to move out of the way a bit as you walk past.

My dress was magical, and because it was so huge I felt lost in it and I loved that. I went dress shopping with my mum and sister and I actually only tried it on as a joke because it was the biggest 'ballgown' in the shop.

My whole life people have said to me, 'You're a big girl,' or, 'You're tall, aren't you?' And do you know what? I walked out of that fitting room wearing that dress and I felt small for once. I felt the best I have ever felt in my life!

To me, everything was just as I wanted it on the day, even down to the little fans I ordered from eBay to use as wedding favours. I added bows and they looked so pretty.

It looks like a lavish wedding but we were on a budget and we planned it right down to the last penny. In the end we only went over it by £27, and Jamie and I did that together and felt proud of ourselves.

When we were organising everything we had a spreadsheet that we updated every Sunday. It had a traffic light system to let us know what had been paid, what hadn't and what we'd paid a deposit on.

We really enjoyed keeping our spreadsheet up to date and it meant things didn't feel overwhelming. It was a great focus for my mind too, and when the wedding was over I missed the planning. Then, shortly after our wedding, @mrshinchhome hit one million followers and my home and my Hinchers became my new focus. And, of course, we had our honeymoon to look forward to.

The honeymoon in the Maldives was the best ten days of my life and I am so grateful for being able to experience paradise like that. Jamie and I saved so hard for it, as we have for everything. Nothing has ever been handed to us but we find we are always saving towards something. Saving for our house deposit, the wedding and then the honeymoon! And now we are saving for an extension on the house.

We're not out for dinner every night or buying expensive clothes, and it's another reason I love a bargain so much. If I get something cheap it means the money I've saved can go towards other things.

It's lucky that we both love being indoors so much, because we save a small fortune by not going 'out out'. We prefer to stay in and watch a film together and have a takeaway, and we love playing cards. Cheesy, but Jamie really is my best friend.

CHAPTER SEVEN

LET'S TALK
ABOUT ANXIETY

'm still a really big worrier. I worry so much. I can build up a whole scenario in my head that might not ever happen but it can stay in my head all day. You can imagine how frustrating that is. In fact, I'm sure some of you don't have to imagine because you're probably in the same boat.

The great thing in this day and age is that everyone talks more openly about suffering from anxiety or depression or whatever it may be, and by talking about it openly we're helping each other. I love that.

These days, instead of me sitting there worrying myself silly, I'll grab Minkeh or Buddy and clean instead of thinking too much. I'm cleaning out my mind while I'm hinching the house or the car or understairs cupboard. It's a real release for me. Some people go to the gym or they bake cakes, and that's what helps to ease their whirring minds. For me, it's cleaning.

I think a lot of people assume I have OCD, but I don't. I just genuinely enjoy cleaning, organising and feeling good in my home. When the house has been hinched and my wax melts are filling the house with my favourite smells, there's no better feeling for me. I relax and switch off and it's almost like a mini therapy session.

We've all got things we're dealing with, it's a part of life, and it's all about finding ways to manage whatever it is we're struggling with. For me, cleaning is something I've discovered makes me happy.

If someone thinks that's sad, then that's fine. I'm okay with that. When you're doing something you love and achieving a happy outcome at the end of it, like I do with cleaning, it gives your self-esteem a boost, and that can only be a positive thing.

I thought it was just me who felt like that but now I realise how many men and women out there live with anxiety or panic attacks. We are not alone any more. So many people have said that they've discovered cleaning has helped them beyond belief, and it's really helped to turn things around for them. It means the world to me to think I may have been a small part of that. If I could share even a handful of the messages I receive on a daily basis then the world would see just how much we all have in common. Please never feel ashamed. I'm 'quirky' and a little 'out there' apparently, but who cares! That's me! We should all be proud of who we are. If I can get over a million followers for being myself . . . then anyone can!

Now don't get me wrong, it's not all rainbows and sunshine having such a large Instagram account. I still get comments online from people who say it's not healthy for me to be promoting OCD, but that's not the case at all and it isn't the source of my panic. When I open a cupboard or a drawer I do like to make sure things are neat, but I think most people do, and I don't see that as a problem.

I worry and I get anxious over stupid things, like what to wear to a meeting, or missing a train or replying to a message the right way. They're things that are probably never going to be an issue but they'll play on my mind.

Sometimes I'll watch an Instagram story back ten times in a day to make sure I haven't said anything that could be deemed to be offensive, as the last thing I would ever, ever want to do is upset anyone.

My anxiety was never cleaning or tidying based, and I was never cleaning because I was panicking about my house not looking perfect. I just found that by cleaning I could calm myself down if I felt a panic attack coming on.

For instance, when I gave my Harry Potter understairs cupboard a good clear-out it triggered something in me. I used to open the door and feel a bit miserable because it was so full of rubbish, but now it's got hooks and shelves and I really enjoy hoovering it and keeping it nice. I've even put a couple of pictures up on the wall. There isn't a single place in my house now that I dread looking at, and that is so good for my head.

If I've got a lot on and I'm out with Jamie or friends or family, I may not clean at all that day, which shows that I'm not obsessed with it as such. My whole life isn't based on cleaning; it just happens to be something I enjoy hugely.

The age-old saying 'tidy house, tidy mind' really does ring true for me. But at the same time I genuinely don't think it's a bad thing to have stuff out of place because then I get to enjoy putting things away again. If they have a home, I know I can always put them back where they belong. It really is no biggie.

I think people do assume that Hinch Headquarters is perfectly spotless and really neat and tidy 100 percent of the time, but that's so not true. If I've got friends over for a night in, there are plates and glasses everywhere, and I'm certainly not sitting there getting itchy about it. I'll think, 'It's out now but I know where it's going to go later,' and the next day, when I put everything back in cupboards, it does feel nice.

If friends bring their kids round, I'll let them have their toys out and have the run of the place and I love it. It doesn't make me feel at all uncomfortable that there's mess or clutter because at the end of the day those toys are either going home with them, or they're going back to their rightful place.

It's really not a disaster if things are untidy. You've got to be able to enjoy your house even if there is a bit of chaos every now and again.

When I have kids they will be able to have as much stuff out as they like. When I was little I used to set all of my Barbies on the landing and make up homes and rooms for them. I didn't ever do it in my bedroom for some reason. I think I wanted more space!

My Barbie accessories would be everywhere and my mum didn't bat an eyelid. She couldn't even walk on the landing sometimes, but she knew that before I went to bed they would all go back into my Barbie box and be tidied away. I was allowed total freedom to be a kid, and that's what my children will have.

WE SHOULD ALL BE KINDER TO OURSELVES, AND TO EACH OTHER

The main source of my worry has always been what other people think of me, and it's something that is improving with time. For instance, with the whole Instagram thing, all I kept thinking for a long time was, 'Why me?'

The products I use have been around for donkey's years. I remember seeing Zoflora on my nan's sink growing up. I'm not doing anything new or ground-breaking here.

I don't think I'm reinventing the wheel, so that makes me

think that maybe people like my Insta because they like me, and that's hard to get my head around.

I do sometimes think, 'How come people are interested in what I'm doing?' I guess the bottom line is that I've never felt good enough.

As I've mentioned, growing up I didn't like going out much. It was mainly because I was constantly nervous about people's first impressions of me. I was scared of talking to them in case I said or did the wrong thing. Confrontation petrifies me.

Even in my late teens I'd go to bars with my friends and everyone would be chatting away, and I felt like as soon as I started talking the whole place would go quiet and everyone would look at me. Of course that wasn't the reality but it was what my insecurity was telling me.

I do still suffer with that side of things, and I probably always will to a certain extent. Sometimes things feel overwhelming and I just have to wait for the mood to pass.

For instance, on the flight back from my honeymoon I had the worst panic attack I've had in years. I'd just had the most amazing time and I had so many incredible things going on in my life, and yet here I was in a pit of despair with a blanket over my head, trying to breathe properly, and I had nothing to pin it on.

I like flying, so it wasn't anything to do with that, and it was really confusing. I did wonder if it was the sudden realisation of how much things had changed for me in the last year.

Most people on the plane were asleep, including Jamie,

and I didn't want to wake him up, but by taking some deep breaths and telling myself everything was going to be okay, I managed to calm down again.

That episode showed me that it's possible I'll always have moments like that, and it's about managing them.

I bumped into some Hinchers on my honeymoon (how crazy is that?) and one of them asked me how I feel now I'm famous, and that was such a shock for me. The word 'famous' makes me think of singers and film stars, not me cleaning and messing around in my house in Essex.

I don't mean that in a 'little old me' way. I genuinely mean that I do not feel in any way famous, and I don't think I ever will. I'm just doing my best in life and I still don't understand what all the fuss is about.

To me, I've got one of the most boring lives going. I don't really have a big hobby or an amazingly interesting job, so I didn't think anyone would be that interested in watching what I do. I still can't believe it. Some people have been on a bit of a journey with me. They've followed me from the very, very beginning when I only had a couple of thousand followers, so they know I haven't changed what I'm doing.

Some of the stories I've heard about myself are hilarious. I have to laugh. When the negative comments first started, I used to physically shake like I was cold. It sounds mad but I'd be so upset about the untrue things that were said. I found it really hard to deal with.

One day, someone said that I was very sad, pathetic, unwell and needed a life because of all the cleaning I do. My mum said to me, 'Soph, if anyone sends you messages like this you don't have to text them back' (she's not very Instagram savvy, bless her). But the concept is the same, I don't need to reply. They don't deserve the acknowledgement and more importantly they are not worth my time. That is valuable hinching time! Ha!

Mum and Jamie both had a good chat with me that evening and said that people who troll other people are probably not feeling great about themselves. I'm not hurting anyone by cleaning my own home, so I don't understand why some people feel the need to be so nasty.

Negative comments still really upset me at times, but I have to think to myself that they're taking time out of their day to watch my videos and then say horrible things about me, which probably means they're quite unhappy.

I know some people are possibly envious of me because of my followers but, like I've said, the irony is that I wouldn't know how to do it again if I tried. It all happened so naturally. A few trolls assume I've bought my followers, but the truth is, I wouldn't even know how, so that's another bit of gossip that has no basis.

Some people think I'm pathetic or stupid for naming my cloths and putting my sink to bed, and I'm constantly reading comments from people saying, 'You're obviously being paid by this company or that company.' But anyone who's followed me from day one will know that I still use the same products now as I did then. I'm loyal to the same brands I've always loved.

Yes, every now and again I will collaborate with people, but I am always, always very upfront and open about that. I'm not trying to trick anyone.

I don't think I'm anything big or special. I'm just doing something that helps my thought processes and hopefully helps other people too. So many people have messaged me to say watching my Instagram posts and stories has changed their lives, which is unbelievable, and makes every bad comment worth it.

I'm such a normal person. I find it so crazy that there are fan pages on Facebook and Instagram.

I think, in the past, I spent about nine hours one day searching every social media platform for my name and reading as many comments as I could find and thinking, 'Wow, that's cruel, that's incorrect, that's a lie, that's offensive!' Why did I look? Why? Then I suddenly realised I'm better off not looking. There is only so much I need to know about what other people are saying about me. It's none of my business, really.

For some reason I thought when I became a bit 'known' (I don't really know how to word it because it sounds a bit cringe) I would toughen up and not care about things. But I didn't suddenly become more resilient. If anything, I became more sensitive and homely and grounded. The last thing I want to do is let any of this run away with me.

I am so, so grateful for everything that's happened to me, but I will always, always be honest about how I'm feeling, and sometimes it feels a bit overwhelming.

I went to Lakeside shopping centre recently and saw a girl

sat on her own eating a packet of crisps, and this may sound ridiculous but I thought, 'I would love her life.' She looked so settled and content. It was lovely to see. It sounds silly but I was really envious of her because, believe it or not, Hinchers, the best lives are the 'boring' ones. The typical everyday routines. Don't envy the life of a 'celeb' or the 'perfect fairy tale', because your best life is probably the one you're living right now. Everything has its positives and negatives.

I've always been close to my friends and family, but since this all kicked off we've become closer than ever. I talk to them every day and they keep me grounded. I feel like as long as they're happy with what I'm doing, everyone else will be. They would be the first ones to tell me if I'd stepped out of line! All I want to do is make them proud.

Having such solid people around me makes all the difference. My friend Georgia is always super honest with me and she said a while back, 'I was worried about you, Soph. I know how much you worry about what people think of you, so this is a hard world for you to step into. I thought it could potentially make you ill. You can't control what other people think of you.' But then she said, 'But I couldn't be more proud of you because it's made you stronger, and this was all supposed to happen for you, you deserve it.' I know when it comes from her it's completely honest and there's no bull, and she is right. I'm still very sensitive but I am learning to deal with it all in a more level-headed way. My best friends know me best.

I don't know how or why things have begun to improve

now, but I think I just got to the point where I couldn't do it to myself any more. I've stopped checking my phone every thirty seconds to see what has been written about me. I've stopped looking and it's so much healthier. I just focus on my Hinchers. They make me so happy.

I also get really panicky about not replying to everyone who messages me but sometimes my inbox is so overwhelming I just can't. I would never, ever want to ignore anyone, but sometimes I'll get over 5,000 messages a day, whether it's a DM or a reply to a story, and you can't physically reply to them all. It would be impossible; I'd wear my fingers down.

I have followers from all over the world now, including Australia, New Zealand, Ireland, Canada, even Iceland! So sometimes I get messages at very strange hours, but I love it.

I put myself under so much pressure to keep on top of things for so long, but in the end I had to throw my arms up and admit defeat, and that's the best thing I could have done for myself. I think people assume I have a team of helpers who reply to everyone, but I really don't. It's just me doing it.

My Hinchers have helped me so much with my confidence. Even when I've been giving myself a bit of a hard time, the way they accept me is amazing.

There are Hinchers of every age, from kids to teens, to men and women in their seventies and eighties, which is so amazing. Some of them really mummy me and ask me if I'm okay all the time, and then I've got other younger girls who say they want to be like me when they're older. It's so sweet.

I love the interaction I have with my followers. I love it

when they help me and pass on tips. When I put polls up people get so involved and it's so helpful. I'm only twenty-eight and I'm still learning about what's right and wrong and what works and what doesn't. I would never tell anyone everything I do is right because it's so not!

I still struggle with feeling I should always be busy. Sometimes I'll sit down and take time out for a few hours and I feel so guilty because I feel like I should be doing a live or posting on my grid or cleaning on my stories. I did a story about going for a bath one day to get away from it all and some people messaged me saying, 'Please just enjoy your bath and put your phone away, Mrs Hinch.' But it's hard.

I think I am beginning to find a good balance now, though. As long as Jamie and I can sit down together every night and have a bit of time where we don't look at our phones, I'm happy. We'll talk about our days and just be Mr and Mrs Hinchliffe, and that relaxes me.

I WILL ALWAYS BE MYSELF

I'm not going to let this run away with me. I've said no to so many working opportunities because they don't feel right and I don't want things to spiral out of control. I want to keep my normal life and be able to wrap up and walk Henry in the park.

The thing is, I absolutely love my life. I have amazing

family and friends, and I've got Jamie and Henry. Jamie and I have some really exciting things coming up, and I love the life we share together. I love, love, love my life the way it is, so why change it?

Now, don't get me wrong, of course if Jamie and I can be better off financially and not have to worry about paying certain bills as a result of everything that's going on, that would be amazing. Who would say no to that? But I don't want it to come at too high a price. I don't want to have to sacrifice what I have. Everything that's happened to me is exciting and lovely, but it hasn't made me any happier because I was already happy before. I just have over a million people to share the happiness with now, and how amazing is that!

Even before the Insta account took off I was living my dream. I was planning our wedding. We'd bought our first home. We had a car we loved and we had a gorgeous fur baby, Henry. I know it sounds so cheesy but life is good because of the people you have around you and how you feel inside; it's not about how big your house is or how much money you have sitting in the bank! Someone said to me recently, 'Why are you still shopping in Poundstretcher? You could be in Harrods.' Well, for a start I couldn't, and secondly, I bloody love Poundstretcher.

It's not like Instagram has made me a millionaire, and I certainly wasn't looking for anything when I started my account. I'm incredibly lucky with what's happened and it's a beautiful thing. But it was never my goal to become well known. I know life would go on without it. But if I can carry on enjoying it and making people laugh, then why not? I want to enjoy it all for what it is.

I know, hand on heart, that this is a Hinch craze and I'm so aware that some day it will calm down and something else will come along to replace it. And when it does, my old life will still be there and it will still be brilliant.

I'm very lucky that I've been offered some fab TV deals, but I'll be honest, I don't want to do that at the moment. I like being the voice and the hand behind my account on Instagram because that's how I feel comfortable, and I wouldn't like it if I became someone that everyone recognised. I don't mind the odd selfie or whatever, but my face everywhere? No thank you, not for me.

I don't want to be criticised or pulled apart, and no matter who you are in the media, that happens. There are women who I think are bloody perfection and even they get trolled, and I don't think I'm strong enough.

I've had people tell me I don't deserve my success or they put me down for the way I look and how I speak, but honestly, the thing that makes me feel better than anything is the positive messages I get from my Hinchers.

Social media can be a tricky place generally and I'm so glad it wasn't around when I was younger. When I see what kids have to go through with it these days, I think it would have killed me. If I'd gone on to Facebook and I'd seen that people were out without me and everyone was tagged, I would have been heartbroken. The FOMO fight is real.

Even now, if I go on to Facebook or Instagram on a

Saturday night and everyone is posting pictures from their evenings out, there is a part of me that thinks, 'Should I be doing that? Am I boring?' But then I curl up to Jamie and cuddle Henry and I know I'm exactly where I want to be.

The thing is, that photo you see of everyone having this amazing time may be the only night out they have that year. We put so much pressure on ourselves to do and be certain things, and sometimes the things we really want are right under our noses the whole time. We're just spending so much time wishing we had someone else's life that we don't realise it.

Social media can also be incredible and positive. What I like most about my account is that it makes people smile. That's a huge part of the reason I do what I do. We're all in this together. Also, being in a position to be able to help small businesses grow and help charities hit their targets is unbelievable.

I think all we're looking for in this life is a bit of happiness and I feel like I've been very lucky and I've found mine. I don't aspire to have a massive house and to go on non-stop holidays – I just want the life I have now.

I don't look at the lives of other people who live in huge mansions and have designer bag collections and wish I had what they do. I really don't need much.

I love what I'm doing, I love my followers, I love life and I love the feeling when I pop off the cap on a new bottle of Zoflora. They are all wonderful things.

DIARY

○ What helps you to feel calm?

....
....
....

○ Are there any smells that soothe your mind?

....
....
....

○ What does your ultimate relaxing bath look like?

....
....
....

○ What is your idea of a perfect evening?

....
....
....

○ What is your favourite book?

....
....
....

○ Do you have a favourite quote?

....
....
....

○ Which one person always makes you feel better when you speak to them?

....
....
....

○ Complete the following: Love is . . .

....
....
....

○ Where is your happy place?

....
....
....

PART FOUR

Grab Your Minkeh, We're Going On A Cleaning Adventure

CHAPTER EIGHT

LET'S CRACK
ON AND
HINCH!

don't ever tell people what they have to clean every day, week or month. There is no set routine in this book, because the truth is . . . I don't have one.

Every morning I like to go and have a little scout around the house and I'll think, 'That could do with a little dust,' or 'I need to hoover in here.' As long as I get it done that day, I'm happy. I want to enjoy it and I certainly don't want to put the pressure of an every-day cleaning routine on myself.

Ideally I like to hoover, dust with Dave, clean the floors,

pine my toilets and wipe over all kitchen surfaces daily, and as an example, I do a deep bathroom clean, wash out the bin and change the beds once a week.

The microwave and oven get cleaned every one to two weeks, and the fridge, curtains, washing machine and inside the kitchen cupboards get a going-over every month.

I also turn and freshen my mattress every month, and every six months I clear my wardrobe out, vacuum pack and store away what I don't need (more tips to come on that in a minute).

If you're cleaning to calm yourself down, the last thing you want to do is put a load of pressure on yourself and think you have to be perfect. You don't have to say to yourself, 'I must do this,' or 'I must do that.'

I go round the house every day and make a list of what I want to do and I take it from there. I'm not that rigid with it. I compartmentalise it (that is one of those words that is so hard to say!) by doing it as and when something needs attention.

EXAMPLE HINCH LIST

TO DO LIST

	Hinched
o Washing	☐
o Pine toilets	☐
o Hoover	☐
o Mop the floors	☐
o Zoflora surfaces	☐
o Put stuff away on bed	☐
o 1001 the carpets	☐
o Clean sink	☐

I'm a very visual person and once I've written everything down my head is no longer going, 'You've got to do this, this and this,' which feels overwhelming. Once it's in front of me it feels manageable. That feeling when you tick something off is so satisfying too.

I can see that I've achieved something, rather than just letting it float around my head, making me worry that I'll forget. You'll notice I'll never say, 'It's bathroom Tuesday today,' or 'It's bedroom Friday.' That's why I have my checklist notepads, because then I can write down everything that I think needs some attention that day.

If I do have a day when I'm not feeling great – and let's face it, we all have them – and I don't want to do that much, I will go back through my pad and look at all of the things I've achieved.

If I'm having a day when I'm feeling particularly unmotivated, I switch things up! Literally! So I won't write down a to do list per say, but I will do whatever I feel up to around the house – no matter how big or how small – and write it down after I've completed it! So it's basically a backwards hinch list! You'll be surprised how much you are getting done without even realising it on those unmotivated days. I was shocked once when I knew it was a backwards checklist day and I looked at what I'd achieved – I did more on that day than on some other days when I've been hinch mad! So remember to give yourself credit. It's so important!

CHAPTER NINE

TIME TO SHINE OUR SINKS AND EASE OUR MINDS

Hinch Haul Heaven!

et's release some of that anxiety and worry with a good solid cleaning sesh! I always find that doing something I love, and doing it well, gives me a real boost. So we're going to get those loos (and showers and fridges!) looking lovely. Then we can sit back and appreciate all our hard work with a cup of tea and a biscuit. Or two.

HINCH YOURSELF HAPPY

A lot of my Hinchers ask me where I get all of my energy to hinch as much as I do. What motivates me most is picturing the end result and the sense of achievement I feel once I've finished cleaning. It's not always easy to get up and get going, and if you're having a slow day, or a low day, and you need some motivation to get you started, here are some tips:

1) You already know about the backwards hinch list – try giving that a whirl!

2) Put some tunes on! Nothing will get you going like your hinch playlist. Music can lift our spirits and soothe our souls, and when I'm feeling low it can pull me out of a bad mood and get Trace and me going!

3) All my Hinchers say that once they start with Zoflora they can't stop. I'm exactly the same! (A bit like Pringles: once you pop, you just can't stop!) The smell is so homely and fresh, once you've started in one room you soon want the smell in every other room in your home.

4) Take photos of your achievements! When I go back and look at the results on my Instagram, it motivates me to go into my bathroom and make it sparkle. Look back on the photos of your home when it's lovely and clean and this will motivate you

to get going. Create your own Instagram account as a personal catalogue of your own success. This can even be a private account if you don't want to share it, but, trust me, the photographs of your perfectly hinched home will inspire you to get started!

5) Don't forget to hinch yourself first! You are just as important as your fresh-smelling home. Whether it's having a long shower, applying your make-up or making yourself a nice cup of tea, focusing on yourself first is an important step before you ready, set, hinch!

BATHROOM

HINCH YOUR BATHROOM

○ I always start off by removing everything that isn't attached, so any ornaments, towels and products come straight out. I clear everything out of the shower, bath and any shelves and put the bath mat in the washing pile.

o Spray down all the tiles with
   Astonish Mould and Mildew Spray.

o Spray Viakal on the taps,
   shower heads and plugs, and
   the shower door. It's fabulous
   for limescale and the shine it
   leaves is the best.

o While that's all doing its job,
   I make a start on my bath using
   Minkeh, and then out comes the
   Flash Bathroom, of course – liquid
   or spray version.

o Once you've finished the bath,
   don't forget to rinse away the
   Viakal from the shower head and
   taps because if left for too long
   it can cause damage.

o Any bathroom shelves and
   surfaces are next, making sure
   I rinse out Minkeh in between.
   I get right into the corners of
   everything because that's where
   the really nasty stuff is hiding.

○ I like to attack the shower with my SonicScrubber (aka Stewart) to clean the plughole, taps or hard-to-reach places in and around the shower door. The sense of satisfaction is unbelievable.

○ Rinse everything off the tiled walls and floor of the shower and bath using the shower head if you can. The smell and shiny results at this exact point are what I love! I leave everything to air-dry, apart from the shower doors and windows. I'll always finish those off with the Minky window and glass cloth (aka Kermit, as we all know him). However, for extra perfection my window vacuum (Victor) is perfect for a streak-free finish on all glass!

○ Next, it's time to attack the toilet. Cif Power and Shine Wipes never let me down when cleaning the toilet, but also I like to use bleach to clean it all over when I feel like it needs a bit more than a wipe!

○ It sounds obvious but don't start on the rim of your toilet, start with the lid because it will be cleaner than the rest of it.

○ Lift the lid and seat and squeeze some toilet cleaner around the toilet rim and leave it to marinate for a while. Harpic Pine is my fave as you all know. Also check that your rim blocks are still intact and change them if needed. They can be very unhygienic if left for longer than they should be.

○ Toilet brush! I pour a neat capful of Zoflora into my toilet brush once it's been cleaned and disinfected just to keep the smell fresh! Every time I use my toilet brush it smells of Mountain Air Zoflora! I mean, who wouldn't love that!

○ If you've got a towel-rail radiator like I have, wipe it down with a dry tumble dryer sheet first to remove any dust. Then pop some Cif Stainless Steel Spray on to a microfibre cloth and wipe it down one rail at a time. Finally, buff it up with Kermit if needed.

o Dave all your skirting boards. Always get rid of the dust before cleaning the floors. (I use my handheld hoover at this point to make sure there really is no dust left over.) The worst combo is dust mixed with a freshly mopped floor! No, mate!

o Use floor wipes, spray mop or a good old mop and bucket to make sure you get every bit of dirt up. I love using diluted Zoflora for this. The smell is divine!

o Stand back, and admire your work!

Bathroom Storage

Now I don't have bathroom cabinets, I've got grey wicker baskets in both of my bathrooms. I store things like my deodorant, toothpaste and Jamie's contact lenses in them – so everyday things. They're easy access. I get pretty ones with the material on the inside and bows on the outside so they don't look too much like storage. They are nice to look at.

I've also got a three-drawer storage unit from The Range which was around £25. It's the home to my beauty products and such, like shampoo, conditioner, shower gels, bath salts and razors, etc. I don't like having bottles lined up in the shower or around the edge of the bath. I find that if you leave them in the shower, soap and scum builds up around them and they can look a little untidy!

Towels

I keep any towels I'm not using in the airing cupboard rather than let them pile up in the bathroom, and I roll them rather than folding them because that way they're easier to stack. Of course they all get sprayed with Febreze after they've been washed.

I change my hand towels every few days and they're so easy to wash and dry. I like to wash large bath towels once they've been used once or twice, but I'll make a call on it depending on how they look and smell (true story).

If I've bathed Henry (he's got his own towel), or if Jamie comes back from football and he's sweaty and muddy, I'll obviously change those towels as soon as they've been used.

Pixie Stamp

I love how we're all now looking at our toilet rolls in such a different light! Toilet roll doesn't have to be boring. I picked up this #pixiestamp technique from @pixiedustcleaninguk. Okay, so this isn't an *essential* cleaning tip, but it does look amazing if you've got people coming to stay.

- Take the first sheet of paper on the roll and fold the right corner on to the left edge. Fold the left corner to the right corner so it forms a triangle shape.
- Make sure your bathroom tap is slightly wet underneath.
- Dab the end of the triangle with the tap so it creates an imprint on the sheet and it then sticks it to the rest of the roll. This is called a #pixiestamp.
- Obviously the toilet roll should always be positioned so you pull the sheets from the top and not underneath. What kind of person pulls it from underneath?
- Pop it back on to the holder and enjoy the fancy vibes.

KITCHEN

HINCH YOUR FRIDGE

○ Empty everything out of the
fridge. Check the use-by dates
and make sure there's no out-of-
date food. That's the worst!

○ If you have any baskets in your
fridge, like I do for things like
sauces and cheese, empty those
too, and fill them with Fairy
Platinum and warm water and
leave to soak.

○ Take the fridge shelves, racks
and drawers out and pop them
in the sink to soak, or if you have
an oven rack soaking tray like I do,
then pop them in there instead, it
works a treat! Again Fairy Platinum
works so well for a soapy and

bubbly cleaning solution. Avoid using neat disinfectants or kitchen cleaners in the fridge as they may contain certain chemicals that could cause contamination.

o Personally, I take out my large vegetable drawer, which is usually sat at the bottom of the fridge, and fill it with Fairy Platinum and warm water. Then I chuck Minkeh in there, squeeze him out and get to work on the inside of the fridge. It works just as well as a huge washing-up bowl would and helps keep the area free from water spilling everywhere!

o There are often marks at the very back of the fridge where labels get stuck or things spill, so I'll put some Pink Stuff on my Minkeh and scrub them away.

o Wipe down the baskets, shelves, drawers and racks after they've been soaked and simply leave them to air-dry!

o Wait until everything is completely dry before putting it all back together. Don't forget to wipe and return your fridge liners. I bloody love those things!

o Last but not least, put the food back. What a pretty sight that is!

TOP TIP:

- Upper shelves: drinks and ready-to-eat foods
- Door shelves: condiments, juices, water
- Lower shelves: eggs, dairy, raw meat
- Bottom fridge drawer: fruit, veggies (but keep separate from each other)
- Never refrigerate: tomatoes, onions or potatoes

Freezer

I don't feel like the freezer needs hinching that often. Most freezer food is contained in some way, so you're not likely to get a lot of spills.

Whenever I do a really big shop to fill the freezer up I'll naturally look through what's already in there and throw out anything that has gone out of date. I'll also move the older food to the front of the freezer so I know to use that first.

Beware of unnecessary boxes because they can take up so much room. Obviously, if you're as good as I am in the kitchen you need to keep food boxes so you've got the cooking instructions. But if you've got a huge box of ice lollies and your kids eat them all, you may only have one left and yet you've got this giant box taking up a ton of freezer space. In that instance, take the contents out, recycle the packaging and write the use-by date on the plastic packet of the actual food with a Sharpie.

I also find that ice-cube bags take up so much less space than trays. If you've got a massive ice-cube tray with only two ice cubes left in it that's so annoying and a waste of much-needed space. I also like reusable plastic ice cubes, especially the light-up ones when you're in the garden with friends in the summer.

Under the Kitchen Sink Narnia

It's so weird that under-sink cupboards are where most of us store our cleaning products, but they can be some of the dirtiest, most neglected and disorganised cupboards of all. People often forget to clean under there because they think, 'Oh, it's just cleaning stuff, how dirty could it possibly be?' but I give mine a good going-over every few weeks.

I've made my cleaning cupboard a joyful place to be for my products by not overloading it (obviously it helps that I have a big Narnia in the garage).

If you overload a cupboard and it's a mess you almost don't want to use it. You'll end up looking at something you don't like every single day and that can make you feel negative.

If I look and there are things falling over each other or there's grime on the floor it will put me in a bit of a bad mood. As my Hinchers know, baskets are a must-have in your Narnias. I have so many self-adhesive hooks, along with the magical tea towel clips that hang our cloth babies and are easily found on eBay.

Honestly, those things can take minutes to do and the payoff will be that lovely feeling of cupboard happiness when you open the door, which is so worth it. Especially as I open mine on average twenty times a day! My bad!

Bins

Kitchen bins are some people's least favourite things to clean but it does need to be done regularly or it can make your kitchen smell so bad. Here's how I clean mine:

HINCH YOUR BIN

- Start off by spraying the whole bin down inside and outside with a disinfectant. I am in love with the Astonish Germ Clear Disinfectant with pine oil! The smell is life! Don't forget to do the lid and the foot pedal too if you have one, because they are often the grubbiest bits.

- I then use an old Dishmatic to give it a good scrub. Because it's small you can get right into the corners and the handle makes reaching the inside of the bin so much easier! You can never have a bin too clean, now can you?

○ Grab your garden hose and use this to shower down any suds. I won't lie, I quite enjoy this part.

○ Keep the lid open and let it air-dry outside.

○ Once dry, bring her inside and pour a capful of neat Zoflora on to some dry kitchen roll and place the kitchen roll at the bottom of the bin before you add a bin liner. Trust me, it will take the edge off any whiffs.

○ You can also pick up some fabulous bin smell-eliminating powders from most supermarkets that are fun to try out! I always pick them up when I see them. Every time I change the bin in between deep cleans, I sprinkle some into the bin bag itself.

Washing Up

I don't own a dishwasher, unfortunately, but I do have my Mr Hinch, who believe it or not actually enjoys washing up! Yes, you read that right! He's so good at it too, which is absolutely fine by me. He says he finds it quite therapeutic, which is handy because I'm not keen on it.

However, when Derek the Dishmatic and I do wash up, these are a few simple steps we follow:

- Always start with your glasses and mugs (or the least dirty items first), then go on to cutlery next.
- Always do your plates and pots last as they are normally the dirtiest thing!
- Keep an eye on the water and be sure to change it before it gets too murky – you can't get clean plates from dirty water.
- Leave your washing up to airdry on the drainer because sometimes tea towels can be muck magnets.
- Always shine your sink at the end and the whole job's a good'un!

HINCH YOUR PLUGHOLES

_____

- Boil your kettle.

- Pour three-quarters of a cupful of soda crystals down the plughole and leave for two to three minutes.

- Fill a cup full of white vinegar and pour this down also. It'll fizz up like a mini potion but that's the best part! Leave it for ten minutes.

- Then pour down a neat capful of Zoflora and leave for one minute.

- Last but not least, pour the whole kettle's worth of boiling water down the plughole to wash it all away!

  Your plugholes will never smell dodge again!

Toaster

Please remember to always unplug your toaster before hinching it! My favourite combo for cleaning the toaster is the Brian cloth and some Elbow Grease.

- Wipe away any visible surface crumbs with a damp cloth.
- Take the little tray out of the bottom and either use Shelley, if you have her, to hoover up all the crumbs or simply tip them in the bin.
- Wash the tray and, while you're working on the rest of the toaster, leave to air-dry.
- Spray Elbow Grease straight on to your cloth and never into the toaster. At the end of the day, your food is going to go in there.
- Using the cloth, wipe away all marks, smudges and smears.
- Once dry, reassemble by putting the crumb-collecting tray back.

Laundry

I use a combo for my laundry and keep them all together in one basket under the sink. My laundry must-haves are:

- Lenor Spring Awakening Fabric Conditioner
- Ariel Gel

- Lenor Unstoppables Fresh In-Wash Scent Boosters
- Astonish Oxy Active Plus Stain Remover

I know that seems like a lot but I do like to take good care of my clothes.

Don't forget to wash your cloths regularly too. You've got to clean the cleaners. The cloths are our babies! You can imagine the germs and dirt that gather on your cloths and sponges after they've been working hard for you.

You can either put them through a 60° or 90° wash (cloth type dependent) with washing gel only (no softener) or:

- Pour a neat capful of Zoflora into your sink and fill with boiling water.
- Chuck your cloths in and leave overnight.
- In the morning, squeeze them out.

The smell fills the room too! Try it if you haven't already and thank me later.

Washing Machine

I hinch my washing machine regularly. Come on, it takes care of our clothes so we should take care of it back. And think about it, if it's dirty it's not going to get your clothes very clean, is it? But don't worry, it doesn't have to be boring! I quite enjoy it!

HINCH YOUR WASHING MACHINE

---

o The first thing I do is put a tea towel
  on the floor in front of the machine.
  May sound so silly and minor, but it
  stops so much 'after mess'.

o All washing machine drawers, where
  we put the washing liquid, powder
  and fabric softener, should slide
  out, and will definitely need a clean
  to remove all the build-up.

o Remove the drawer and put
  it in your sink. Spray it down with
  your favourite multi-purpose cleaner
  and leave it to soak whilst you
  tackle the rest of the machine.

o Spray your chosen washing
  machine cleaner or similar inside the
  drawer hole. You'll be surprised how
  much builds up in there. I also use
  my electric SonicScrubber at this

point to get right inside the hard-to-reach places!

o Pull back the rim on the front of the washing machine and spray down. Again, you'll be surprised by what you find in there. If you're lucky you may come across a few quid. I know some people probably take the entire rim off the door to clean it but I'd be too scared that I wouldn't get the thing back on again, so this quick washing machine clean is enough for me.

o Get a moppet sponge (Pinkeh) and wipe out deep inside the rubber rim – it hides the most dirt!

o You then want to give the washing machine window a nice shine so any glass cleaner works really well for this.

o Rinse and dry your washing machine drawer and fit it back in place.

- Now it's time to clean out your poor washing machine's insides! Add three tablespoons of bicarbonate of soda to the drawer and a cupful of white vinegar to the drum of the machine and run the machine on a 90° wash. This helps remove mould and mildew, detergent build-up and any unwanted odours. (Don't forget to chuck the Pinkeh and floor tea towel you've just used in the drum too, whilst you're at it.)

- Give the front of the washing machine itself a little spritz of diluted Zoflora spray just because we can!

- Don't forget, Hinchers, you need to check your washing machine filter. This only needs to be done every three months or so, but do try and keep on top of it because it will make a huge difference to your laundry. You'll be shocked with what you find in there, from hair clips and collar plackets to pound coins and buttons.

Tumble Dryer

My tumble dryer is my saviour. It's so simple to use and everything comes out fluffy and smelling lovely.

I was so shocked when I first discovered all the fluff that had built up in my tumble dryer. At the end of the day, tumble dryers and toasters are both appliances that heat up so they can be dangerous, and you need to really keep on top of them.

When you open the tumble dryer there is usually a little handle inside the door. If you lift your handle up you'll find the filter and I bet you it's full of fluff and fibres from towels and clothes.

I empty the filter after each use and gather up all the fibres and pop them into a bin I've got next to my tumble dryer.

The only things I don't tumble dry are Jamie's shirts. They'll go on hangers and I'll pop them on to hooks on the back of a door to air-dry.

I'll be honest, I hate ironing so I don't really do it. It's one of my worst jobs alongside washing up, so I do take Jamie's shirts to a local pressing shop. They iron them for me, pop them back on my great bargain eBay hangers and I whisk them home. I feel very guilty but I cannot lie about it!

I may be kidding myself but I don't think many of my clothes need to be ironed. I'll pop them in the tumble dryer or hang them up and the creases seem to fall out. Plus, if you're wearing stretchy material or skinny jeans they kind of iron themselves on your body, surely? I've managed to get away with that logic for years.

I also really do rate the natural reusable wool tumble dryer balls! It saves your dryer from the residue left from liquid fabric softeners, shortens the drying time AND keeps pet hair off clothes. They can be ordered on eBay, guys!

Let's Cut Down On All Of This Ironing Malarkey

Little and often is my advice to you, fellow Hinchers! To me there's nothing more intimidating than a towering ironing pile. If you let it build up, it becomes a much more daunting task and seriously scary!

- Small loads on short and sweet cycles are key when it comes to tumble drying! This is because there's less in there so the clothes don't crease as much. If you have the option on your machine, a cooler setting is also better for preventing the creases from setting. It works for me, Hinchers!
- Before ironing, lightly spritz your clothes with diluted fabric softener. This not only smells amazing

but it helps the creases drop out and makes the boring task of ironing more bearable.

- With heavier garments, like shirts, jumpers, jumpsuits and dresses, hang them immediately after they've been washed, as the weight of them pulls the creases out whilst drying. Let gravity do its thing!
- Always check the labels in clothes for ironing guidelines – I cannot begin to explain how many items of clothing I have literally burnt in the past (embarrassing, I know!).

Oven

As people know, I don't have Jamie Oliver quaking in his boots when it comes to cooking. But that doesn't mean I don't give it a go sometimes, so my oven does need cleaning regularly. I personally find a quick oven clean regularly is more enjoyable than a serious deep oven workout every month. Once again, little and often is key.

I've got my crock-pot and when I've had kids I'd like to be just like my mum and make the most lovely meals for people. The problem is, she's always cooked for me so I've never had the need to – I know that's so bad. I do try to make Jamie nice dinners, and I always make sure he's got something to eat when he gets home because he often gets in late. I'm lucky that Jamie is so easily pleased with food! I mean, his favourite meal of all time is tuna pasta with salad. I rest my case!

We still go to my mum's for a roast every Sunday and we love it. She even makes Henry a chicken dinner too! My mum's food is the best food you can get; I would rather go to hers than a fancy restaurant any day of the week. I don't know what I would do without her!

Talking of cooking, can I just point out that even though I have a vase of flowers on my hob, I do move them when I cook. They're not there permanently. People always mention them, but they do get repositioned to the dining table when I'm getting my cook on! All the best!

HINCH YOUR OVEN

○ Take the oven racks out, fill up
  the sink with warm soapy water,
  and spray the racks with Fairy
  Power spray. Leave them to soak.
  This particular spray is fab for
  removing grease spills and
  stains.

○ Remove your oven liner if you
  have one (if you don't, I really
  recommend you buy one – cheap
  but works a treat). Spray this also
  with Fairy Power spray and leave
  to do its thing.

○ I personally start by using an old
  dry paintbrush to brush away any
  crumbs or food that may have fallen
  into the door crevice and gaps. You'll
  be surprised how much falls away
  with such little work! It can sometimes
  look worse than it is! My mum swears

by an old solid paintbrush, bless her, and now I do too!

o You'll then need to use something more abrasive! I use Pink Stuff, but of course there are many alternatives. I find the Astonish range of oven paste cleaners are also fab! Now get a tough scouring sponge (I use the Scrub Daddy sponge for this) and start working the paste into the stubborn spots.

o Little Tip: If you would rather not use a paste cleaner you could always sprinkle a generous amount of baking soda over the stubborn burned spots. Next, spritz some white vinegar over the baking soda. Sit back and watch the mini science project that'll appear in your oven! Let this bubble for a while, maybe thirty minutes or so.

○ Pop an old tea towel on the floor in front of the oven door to protect your floor from that gooey oven juice (yuck).

○ Once the stubborn spots have been removed or loosened, rinse and wipe away with a cloth and a bowl of warm water mixed with Fairy Platinum. You may need to rinse and wipe thoroughly a few times. I advise investing in an oven/hob scraper for those tougher burnt-on stains – I picked up on this little tip from @littlemissmops on Instagram and they can easily be found on eBay!

○ While this is air-drying from the inside out, get back to your racks! Rub them down with your choice of tough sponge and the stubborn marks should simply wipe away. Lift them out of the sink to air-dry.

- Don't forget to dry the rubber door seal with some kitchen roll too! That builds up dirt like you wouldn't believe.

- Spray the outside of your oven door with a germ killer and disinfectant spray and wipe away.

- Then spray your glass door with your favourite glass cleaner and buff it up with some dry kitchen roll or even Kermit, if you have him.

- When both the racks and the liner are dry, slip them back into the oven and that's it! You're ready to whip up a five-course gourmet meal (or stick a ready meal in, of course).

Hob

I do this as and when it needs cleaning. If you cook every day, it'll need this little clean every day!

I like the winning combo of Cif Original Cream Cleaner and my Minkeh for my hob! It's never let me down and I'm in love with the after-shine.

Kitchen Cupboards

I'm really good at going through most of my cupboards, but it's easy to forget about those ones that we use to house the things we really don't need (you know, like cake tins and a juicer we've used once).

I was so shocked when I went through my cupboard of doom where old things go to die. I had no idea how much stuff I was storing in there, and none of it was anything I needed. Who needs old Tupperware with no lids or a cheese grater that doesn't work properly?

I ditched all the stuff I didn't need and it felt amazing. I hinched it by filling it back up with the stuff I did want to keep, and organising it so it looked lovely. Admittedly, I then had a little extra spare room in that particular cupboard so it now houses more Zoflora (oops)!

HINCH YOUR CUPBOARDS

○ Take everything out of the cupboards and push it all to one side of the worktop.

○ Check the sell-by dates of everything and throw out anything that's out of date.

○ Spray a generous amount of disinfectant inside the cupboards and wipe it around with the white side of a Minkeh and allow it to air-dry. This is so quick and easy to do with Minkeh. Another reason why I'm in love with the little man so much.

○ I then check out my beloved food cupboard baskets. I keep ready-to-cook rice and Pasta 'n' Sauce (I'm not going to lie, I love them) in their own little basket. Also my casserole sachets and dumpling mixes, etc, sit in another. My mum has always done this and I've copied her, I guess!

I also have a large white basket I keep at the top of one of my food cupboards: 'the treat basket'. Random, I know, but it works and fits up there perfectly on the shelf. Jamie and I grab the treat basket most evenings, put it in between us on the sofa when we're watching TV and munch away! There's so much in there from tubes of Smarties and Haribos to individually wrapped Mr Kipling cakes and Milky Way crispy rolls! It's a space-saver too, because I empty anything that's a 'treat' or sweet into the basket and recycle the unnecessary boxes they come in.

One of the best things I've bought for the house was a little kid's bookshelf from Ikea. I painted it grey (obvs) and my dad screwed it to the wall, and now my herb pots sit on there along with a little tiny hand-painted jar. It's a storage solution plus a cute kitchen feature in one!

Another brilliant thing I've bought is an extendable shelf organiser from Lakeland, and it's amazing. You stack your tinned food on each of the three shelves so you can see what you've got really quickly and easily. Have you ever tried to balance your beans on top of your chicken soup? Because I have, and I'm telling you now, it's not the one!

○ Little Tip: Put the items that have the longer shelf life at the back, and the ones that need to be used sooner at the front. Always works for me!

○ Always put your mugs and glasses away into the cupboards

with their bottoms in the air so
dust doesn't settle inside.

o Finally, for your plates, I would
recommend a corner kitchen
plate rack for your cupboards.
They are goals! It means you can
separate your plates out into the
right piles and get to the ones
you need without having to wrestle
with the ones on top first!

Hinch Your Sinks

Everyone knows I love to shine my sink and put it to bed – it does literally soothe my soul. My sink is stainless steel, but so many of you Hinchers have messaged me to ask for the best way to shine your own sinks. Be it granite, ceramic or enamel, here are the best tips to hinch your sinks!

SINK	HINCHED
STAINLESS STEEL	For a quick, everyday hinch of your stainless steel sink (or multiple times a day, if you're anything like me), use a disinfectant spray, like Stardrops Pine Disinfectant Spray, aka Paul the Pine, and our Minkeh. Spray the sink all over and use damp Minkeh's white belly to scrub the product into the surface area. Don't forget to give Minkeh a good squeeze to release any soaked up product. Who doesn't love all those suds? Once you've rinsed the product away, use Minkeh's green, honeycomb side to soak up any excess. I love to go in the direction of the draining board slats. I just find it so satisfying!

Then out comes the star of the shiny sink show! Stainless steel spray, aka Cliff the Cif. Spray Cliff all over the sink and leave him for a few minutes to work his magic. Now you need to grab Buddy! I find that he works best when he remains that little bit damp (could have been worse, Hinchers . . . I could have said moist again, haha!). Use Buddy to buff the stainless steel spray into the sink. And then stand back and admire that shine. R-E-S-P-E-C-T! If you know, you know!

For a more thorough sink hinch, substitute Paul the Pine with Cif Original Cream Cleaner. Actually, let's be honest, Hinchers . . . I do this step as well, because you know I just love the smell of pine. You can't beat it!

If you find yourself with stubborn stains on your sink that just won't budge, crack open a bottle of Bar Keepers Friend. It's a powdered substance that you turn into a paste by adding a small amount of water. I like to use mine with Scrub Daddy to really work the substance into the surface.

	Make sure you read the labels and follow the instructions because it's strong and can cause damage if used inappropriately. But when used properly, it is so effective.
	If you prefer a more natural, deep-clean method, use a bicarbonate of soda paste (made up of soda crystals, water and white vinegar). It cleans without scratching, and also leaves a fab, shiny finish!
CERAMIC	Butler or Belfast sinks are usually ceramic and if you've got one of these you'll want to take care of it and keep it looking beaut so that the glaze doesn't craze, chip or scratch. So here we go: 1) Scrub-a-dub-dub with Derek the Dishmatic and warm soapy water or a Cif cream cleaner. 2) Use Minkeh to wash the suds away and, for a really amazing finish, disinfect afterwards with the one and only Paul the Pine. 3) Also, make sure you've got a mat or plastic washing-up bowl to protect the surface in the long run.

ENAMEL	Fairy Liquid and my mate Minkeh are all you need for the everyday care of your enamel sink. Top tip: never use scourers or chlorine bleach to clean your enamel, as they'll scratch and dull the surface. For tough to remove water marks and stains, sprinkle on some baking soda, a few drops of hydrogen peroxide and scrub with a non-abrasive sponge.
GRANITE AND COMPOSITE	Minkehs at the ready! My motto is to clean little and often to keep everything tip top. This is especially true for granite and composite sinks. Use hot but not boiling soapy water, and, of course, your Minkeh to clean this surface. To lift stains use a nylon brush and a 50/50 solution of hot water and white vinegar. Then rinse and dry once the stain has gone. As one of the more sensitive surfaces, remember not to leave your sponges and cloths in it overnight as they can leave marks! Also, it's best to keep away from bleach, ammonia or spray cleaners and wire brushes as they can damage this surface.

BEDROOM

Mattress

As you know, each day the beds are made and sprayed with Febreze, but you need to turn and refresh your mattress once a month, guys. And here's how to do it!

HINCH YOUR MATTRESS

○ Completely strip your bed down to its naked self!

○ Hoover your mattress to within an inch of its life; you'll get rid of all the dead skin cells and dust.

○ Using a flour sieve, shake bicarbonate of soda evenly all over the mattress – remember this amazing stuff is an odour eater.

○ Leave for a few hours at least and then hoover it off – it will lift out any nasty whiffs. Especially if you have kids that have had an accident in the bed! Urine smell . . . see ya later, mate!

DUVET HINCH

Let's face it, we all hate changing duvet covers. Well, I certainly do! I think the quickest way to change your duvet is to turn the quilt cover inside out, pop your hands into the inside corners, grab the duvet on the corners and then tip the duvet cover back on to it. Shake them together until the quilt cover has fallen over the whole duvet and you're done!

It works so well and it's quick, and that's what we all want with this nightmare job. Once the fresh sheets are on, the bed has been made, cushions have been karate chopped, give the whole bed a quick spritz with a spray bottle full of your fave fabric softener and water mix. It smells LUSH! Also remember, once you've washed your bedding, to store your duvet cover, sheet and pillowcases inside one of the pillowcases belonging to the set. That way you'll keep the whole collection neatly together and you won't be hunting around your linen storage on duvet-changing day trying to find any missing pieces!

Bedside Cabinets

Mine and Jamie's bedside cabinets are like his and hers drawers. It's Jamie's man drawer and it's my woman drawer. Obviously we both have our own bits in there, so we'll have our passports and ear plugs, and mine will also have an eye mask and some paracetamol in case I wake up in the night with a headache. There's nothing worse than having to trudge downstairs in the dark to get some.

I swear, Jamie always has old batteries and a couple of screws in his, while mine will have several kirby grips and a random lip balm. Mind you, I seem to find kirby grips everywhere. I must have hundreds around my house. I now collect them all up and keep them in an old recycled candle jar (never chuck your candle jars).

If it gets to the point where the drawers don't open and close easily, I know it's time for a clear-out. I don't know how it happens, but those little drawers seem to magically fill up without you realising.

I've also got my bargain eBay storage baskets in my bedroom, so anything that doesn't fit in my bedside cabinet goes in there.

They are so brilliant for extra storage and they look really pretty stacked in the corner of the room, so if you do run out of space they're such a good idea because you can make a feature out of them.

I've got three stacked up on top of each other, and one of them has my books in, another one has my cosmetics in, and then Jamie gets the small one at the top for his man stuff, like his beard trimmer. It's only fair, he's got much less stuff than me!

MY PRE-BED RITUAL

- I like to spray down my surfaces with my Zoflora mixture and then wipe them over with Pinkeh.

- I give any cloths and sponges I've used that day a bath by putting them in the sink, aka putting the sink to bed. I push the plug down and add a capful of Zoflora and a kettle full of boiling water so they can have a nice soak overnight. It will also make your kitchen smell lovely.

- I make sure my TCS – tea, coffee and sugar, always in that order – canisters are all lined up straight (it's the little things).

- I put a wax melt in my burner ready to put on the following morning.

- I'll put my to do list notebook on the table so it's waiting for me.

○ I put my sofa to sleep by giving it a
  Febreze spritz, making sure
  the blankets are put away and
  the cushions are chopped!

○ I squeeze toilet cleaner down the loos.
  Not every night, though. Sometimes
  I'll pour in the Bloo Foam Aroma
  Ocean instead!! That's a beaut!

It may seem weird doing all of this but it makes me feel so
much calmer. If I know that when I get up the house is going
to be clean and tidy I sleep better. Strange, but true. I wake
up feeling more together and refreshed when I've done my
wind-down routine.

LIVING ROOM

Sofa

Everyone's sofa fabrics are different. I've worked out what
works for mine through trial and error, so always do a patch
test on yours somewhere it won't be seen to make sure it's okay
with the products you're using. My sofa is my pride and joy so
if you're anything like me, I wouldn't want you ruining yours!

HINCH YOUR SOFA

○ Remove all seat and decorative cushions, throws and blankets from the sofa.

○ Check for coins. You don't want to hoover those up. Finders keepers!

○ Hoover up all your unwanted findings, from crumbs to God knows what else that ends up down the sides of the sofa seats.

○ Brush your lint roller over the sofa itself and the seat cushions to pick up any lint and loose hairs. Particularly important step if you have fur babies.

○ Mix warm water, two capfuls of fabric softener and a capful of Ariel Gel in a large bowl.

- Dip a white cloth into the mixture (always white, again to avoid colour transfer) and wring it out as much as possible.

- Wearing your rubber gloves, hold the cloth tight and scrub away at each cushion seat, the sofa arms and the back of the sofa.

- Give it a gentle brush all over using a body brush to help revive the fibres.

- Allow it to air-dry, reassemble and enjoy your sofa's new lease of life!

TOP TIP: I love it when you lean on a cushion and it smells so fresh it's like the scent is trying to escape. Tumble dryer sheets have so many ways of creating this heavenly scent in and around your home. Simply pop a scented tumble dryer sheet into your cushion cover and replace them weekly.

HOW TO HAVE A COSY SOFA

My sofa is the heart of my home. I've had it for five years and I am still so in love with it. I've been offered so many new sofas since my account took off but I love mine too much to part with it.

Jamie and I worked so hard for it. I remember seeing it in DFS and thinking, 'One day that will be mine.' My particular sofa is called the Loch Leven and I didn't want to have to wait until we'd saved up so in the end Jamie and I got it on the pay-monthly scheme because I wanted it so badly. We couldn't really afford it but it's *so* worth it.

Personally, I've always loved a sofa where if you sit right back on it your feet don't touch the ground. When I sit back on my sofa my feet dangle, which makes me so happy – I feel like a big kid again.

I like my sofa to smell of Febreze Spring Awakening so I give it a good spritz every day. It's amazing how the smell surrounds you when you sit down on it. It's like a giant fragrant hug.

I always have an oversized warm blanket in a basket nearby that I can grab, and obviously you need nice big cushions you can karate chop.

Finally, have a Henry! Cuddling him makes me so relaxed.

THE CUSHION KARATE CHOP

This is such a classic. I had seen so many Instagram interior posts of karate-chopped cushions and I remember thinking to myself, 'Those cushions look rather posh. How do I get mine looking like that?' When I first saw how the cushions were shaped that way it looked as if they were being karate chopped, so that was it, the phrase has just stuck with me ever since!

I tried it on some cushions I had at the time but they wouldn't form the nice peaks, no matter what I did. They kept bouncing back up, and then I realised the cushions have to be feather for it to work. If you have wadding-type stuffing, frankly you're stuffed.

Rugs and Carpets

There's nothing quite like a lovely clean-smelling rug, and this particular tip was actually shared on one of my Facebook fan pages by a fellow Hincher (I still can't believe I have actual fan pages, melts my heart!).

HINCH YOUR RUGS

- Pour a capful of your favourite fabric softener and Ariel Excel Washing Gel into a bowl. Add some warm water and give it a good stir.

- Use a white cloth (rugs seem to transfer colour especially easily) and soak the whole cloth in the mixture.

- Rub the cloth over your rug or carpet, working in sections, rinsing your cloth out regularly. This is a serious arm workout, but trust me it's worth it!

- Little Tip: Make sure you have your favourite playlist on in the background for this exercise! Scrub to the beat, babe! Scrub to the beat!

- Then use a hand-held all-purpose scrub brush to revive the surface pile by brushing the rug/carpet back to life.

- Allow it to air-dry, and ta-da! Done!

Lantern Cleaning

Okay, so this one is a bit specific, but tons of us have candle holders or lanterns around our homes these days so I really wanted to do a lantern hinch. (Mainly because I absolutely love them and I think they make rooms look so warm and cosy.)

HINCH YOUR LANTERNS

- Start by getting rid of any dry wax residue using an old credit card. Gently nudge at it until it comes away. I once tried to wipe up wax when it was still in liquid form and it smeared horribly, so I would not recommend that.

- To get the rest of the candle residue off, spray some Elbow Grease and wipe with a Minkeh, or something else that has a slightly rough side.

195

- Clean the top and inside of the lantern. Mine always has a few pet hairs on top and inside it (understandably) and loads of marks (how do they even get there?), so wipe away any loose hairs or dust using a tumble dryer sheet. If you go straight in and try to clean the glass or chrome the chances are it will go all splodgy and you'll just be wiping mess around.

- Spray white vinegar spray on to the whole thing, inside and out.

- Wait, don't use your cloth yet! First get some kitchen roll and rub the spray in.

- Now it's time for the cloth. I use Kermit, and he really shines mine up.

- Pop in some fresh candles and you're good to go.

GENERAL ALL AROUND THE HOUSE TIPS

TOP 5 HINCH SAFETY TIPS

1. As all my Hinchers know, I'm a huge fan of wax melts! But please make sure the fire and smoke detectors are regularly tested. I personally set a monthly reminder in my phone, so I never forget.

2. When using any cleaning products always check and follow the manufacturer's instructions. It's so important to know how to use a product correctly. I know my Hinchers are aware of this, but please no mixing of chemicals – it can be really dangerous!

3. To avoid cross-contamination, colour code your cloths against different rooms in the house. This way, you're not using the same Minkeh to clean your sink that you just used to clean your toilet!

4. Think about where you build your Narnias! We don't want young hands having access to Cliff the Cif and Paul the Pine. If you have young children in your home, store your cleaning products up high or use the cupboard safety catches.

5. Think about your pet's safety when hinching. If it's raining outside I won't do the floors that day because there's nowhere for Henry to wait whilst the floors dry. It's their home too and we want to keep our fur babies safe.

Stain Removal

Stains. Who likes them? No one! Let's be honest, does everyone else just stand there looking at a stain thinking, 'What the hell do I do?' So here's a table to show you what to do with the most common household stains.

STAIN	HINCHED
FLOWER POLLEN	Lilies are the worst for this. If you catch it early, the best thing to do is to use Sellotape to lift the pollen off the fabric. But if the stain has settled, apply a small amount of undiluted detergent to the stain and massage gently with a cloth. Then pop this in the washing machine on a cool rinse setting.
RED WINE	Lift as much as you can with a dry paper towel and then cover the entire stain with salt. Leave the salt to soak in – it will absorb the wine and help to lift the stain. Once dry, simply vacuum everything up.

BLOOD	Soak in cold water immediately. This stops the blood from sinking further into the fabric. As with wine, cover the stain in a thick layer of salt to pull the bloodstain out of the fabric. From there, for any residual staining, use either a stain remover like Vanish or a simple bar of soap and massage gently until the stain is hinched away. Removing dried bloodstains can be a bit trickier; for this you'll need to soak the stain in cold water and a mild detergent overnight.
URINE	Make a paste with bicarbonate of soda and white vinegar. Massage the paste into the problem area and hoover away once the stain has been lifted. Finish off with a spritz of Febreze!
GRASS STAINS	Jamie's football kit is always covered in grass stains - nightmare! For me the one and only way to remove these stains is to use my good old Dr Beckmann stain remover. He never lets me down!
SWEAT STAINS	Soak the item in a mixture of cold water and white vinegar for up to 30 minutes, then wash the clothing in the machine as normal.

WAX	Take a brown paper bag, lay it across the wax stain and simply iron over the top. The brown paper bag will absorb the wax and your carpet or rug will look brand new!
INK	I always advise a patch test for this one. Spray the problem area directly with hairspray and wait for up to 30 seconds before simply wiping the ink away with a clean, damp cloth.
CHEWING GUM	Simply put the item in the freezer for a few hours until the gum hardens. Once the gum is frozen solid, peel it away, but remember to be gentle – you don't want to rip that fabric. If the item in question doesn't fit in the freezer, simply apply an ice cube instead and use this to peel away the gum.
LIPSTICK	Spray Elbow Grease, aka Elvis, directly on to the stain. Once this has soaked in, put through the wash as usual. Elvis will not evaporate in your washing machine, which is why this trick works so well!

Woodwork

I personally love cleaning my woodwork, especially if I'm doing a clockwise clean (info a few pages on!), because woodwork can easily get overlooked.

I don't like to use bleach or anything too harsh on the banisters or skirting boards because I worry they're too near the carpet and I could end up dripping something that damages or discolours the carpet. It could easily happen.

I love doing the trick of using two capfuls of fabric softener mixed with hot water, just enough so it makes the mixture runnier.

I soak my Minkeh in the mixture and attack all the skirting boards, doors, door frames, banisters, dado rails, door bars and radiator covers in my house.

Chandeliers

Chandeliers can be a bit of a nightmare to clean because dust and thunder flies get caught up in them, but if you wipe over the small crystals or the delicate details using a tumble dryer sheet it picks up all the nasties! It's all about the anti-static technology, you see. Picks up everything!

Curtains

I wash my living room curtains once a month. I have the kind that you can bung in the washing machine, so I'll do one at a time with some Ace For Whites or a colour brightener because it makes them really zing.

I'll hang them over the banisters and spray them with diluted Zoflora once they're dry. Once they're back up they smell amazing and they will get sprayed most days! I love my curtains so they deserve it! Ha!

Radiators

I'm not telling you how to suck eggs here, but I'd never heard of a radiator brush myself until recently so I'm just sharing the brush love! I clean the backs of my radiators using the long-handled radiator brush I bought from eBay for around a fiver! It gets behind and cleans the dust in between the rad bars so well. I'll then spray the radiators down with my diluted Zoflora spray and wipe down with Minkeh.

Mirrors, Windows and Glass

Mirrored furniture is so in right now, but those annoying finger prints are not! I find the best way to make all reflective surfaces shine is to follow these simple steps.

HINCH YOUR MIRRORS

_____

- Use a fluffy duster or tumble dryer sheet to pick up any dust on the surface.

- Spray with Astonish Window and Glass or white vinegar if you prefer.

- Use dry kitchen roll to buff it in.

- Finish off with our Kermit window and glass cloth.

- Look at your reflection and think, 'Wow, good job done, mate!'

Airing Your House

I used to think that the best way to air your house was to open the windows and let any unwanted smells out. I also assumed the fresh air would then fly through the house and magically take all the bad smells with it. But no!

I went to the Febreze P&G factory in Brussels last year and it was so exciting. As you know, smells are my thing and I loved seeing how everything was made. I had no idea how much went into cleaning products. The technology was incredible. I met the scientists in the labs and they showed me how everything is created.

I asked them about airing things by opening the windows and they told me that it does help, but actually using something that is odour eliminating like Febreze is going to work so much better (I know they would say that, but bear with me!).

When you open the window the air will pull the smells out of things, but unless you do something to actually get rid of those whiffs they will settle back down into the fabrics. Odour-eating products actually eat the smells, as does bicarbonate of soda. They're like someone with a hangover going to McDonald's – they will literally gobble up everything.

A man called Dr Tohan Thrihn, who was a researcher at P&G, discovered it back in 1994. He was a heavy smoker and when he went home one night his wife asked him if he'd stopped smoking because she couldn't smell it on his clothes.

He had been smoking that day and he couldn't understand it, so he racked his brains to try and work out what could have affected his clothes in that way, and realised it was a chemical that was being used in the lab that he was working in. Cyclodextrin grabbed hold of bad smells and eliminated them. How mad is that?

Febreze was then launched four years later using this technology as a fabric freshener to eliminate odours from fabrics, like mattresses and sofas, etc, and now obviously you can get it in lots of different forms. Febreze . . . I love ya!

I love that story too. My mind was blown!

THOSE LITTLE THINGS YOU MAY FORGET

Vases

Is there actually anything worse than the smell of old flower water? I can't even describe how much I hate it. Also very upsetting is the horrible residue that's left behind in glass vases after your poor flowers wither and die. Simply pour some bicarbonate of soda inside the vase and spray some white vinegar inside. Swill it around and leave for a good few minutes, rinse and air-dry! If you're a fan of artificial flowers, like me, use a tumble dryer sheet to dust over the flowers and pick up any debris. You can also hide a tumble dryer sheet in with your flowers – they can't be seen but they can be smelt!

TOP TIP: Spray artificial flowers with your diluted Zoflora spray and they'll smell like an actual dream!

Light Switches

Don't forget these bad boys, you touch them every day. It's too easy to take them for granted and it makes a huge difference when they're clean.

You don't want to use anything too wet because obviously you're dealing with electricity, so lightly spray your diluted Zoflora mix on to a microfibre cloth and then wipe down the switches.

Your Toothbrush Holder

Come on now, this houses something that goes in your mouth so it's got to be super clean. I make sure I rinse out the pot regularly with bicarbonate of soda and water.

Then I'll put a couple of capfuls of mouthwash in there and leave the toothbrush heads in it to soak. It's got alcohol in it so it cleans them really well. If you do it at least once a week, you'll avoid that horrible residue that can build up on the handle of a toothbrush if it's sat in a toothbrush holder for too long. I do also have an electric toothbrush which I clean with bicarbonate of soda and water. It works a treat!

Easy-Peasy Hinching Squeegee

This hack, especially if you have pets, will never let you down. It's up there with hinching my sink as one of my most satisfying chores. Simply drag the window squeegee over all carpets and rugs to collect all old fibres, pet fur, hair and general day-to-day dirt. However, do not do this too often – once a fortnight is absolutely fine – otherwise you'll cause long-term damage to your carpets. None of us want bald carpets now, do we!

Pots and Pans

Have you ever turned one of your pans over? Mate, they're a disgrace if left too long.

HINCH YOUR PANS

- Cover the bottom of your pan in Fairy Power Spray and leave for five minutes to give it a chance to dissolve the dirt.

- Rinse away.

- Rub on a thick layer of The Pink Stuff or a paste cleaner of your choice and, using Scrub Daddy, scrub away generously until the underneath of your pan is shiny again.

- Then rinse away using washing-up liquid and allow to air-dry.

- Hinchers, don't forget to post your before and after pics of your hinched saucepans. I love seeing your results!

TV

You have to be really gentle with your TV. Anything you use that's really wet will smear terribly and could harm the screen.

I would recommend using Pledge Electronic wipes because obviously they're made especially for TVs. They're also brilliant for computers, laptops and remote controls.

Your Mobile Phone

That thing is being touched, either by your hands or your ears, all day long. So show it some cleaning love!

You can either use the electronic wipes mentioned above, or spray a little bit of diluted Zoflora on to some dry kitchen roll and then give the front and back a quick once-over.

Toilet Brush

I have toilet brushes in both of my bathrooms but I only buy cheap ones because I like to replace them really often for very, very obvious reasons.

If I do find a nice plastic one I'll always pick it up, because the metal ones tend to rust. Plus, they're more expensive so you'll probably be more loath to throw them away.

Remember: to make them that bit nicer, I put a capful of

neat Zoflora in the bottom of the holder. At least that way when you pull out the brush you get a nice waft of fragrance.

Wooden Blinds

I wanted to include this because I get asked a lot about how I hinch my blinds. Cleaning your blinds can appear a little tricky to do at first as they are delicate and fragile, but here are a few simple steps to make it easy!

HINCH YOUR BLINDS

- Close the slats shut and give it the once-over with your favourite duster (aka Dave!). Then turn the slats in the other direction and repeat.

- Wipe over each slat with a tumble dryer sheet as the anti-static technology picks up the more stubborn dust.

- Add some diluted Zoflora to some dry kitchen roll and wipe over again.

- Leave to dry.

Kettle

We all have a Kimberly Kettle in our lives, but do you hinch it the way you should? 'Cause, mate, the limescale that builds up can seriously affect your cuppas!

HINCH YOUR KETTLE

- Half fill your kettle and boil it.

- Unplug it or remove it from its stand.

- Pour in your preferred kettle descaler, following the measuring guides on the back of the product.

- Leave it for the recommended time.

- Watch in wonder as all the dodgy bits start floating around.

- Empty the kettle.

- Refill it halfway and boil again.

- Once it's boiled pour the water out, and she's good to go!

Cutlery Drawer

I was having a nightmare with my cutlery drawer until I discovered drawer dividers. All of the trays you can buy in the shops are too wide for my drawer because it's only small, but now I've got the dividers from eBay everything is laid out exactly as I want it.

I've got all my small cutlery in one drawer, and then all of my larger utensils are in another drawer. I don't like them being out on display because they're dust collectors.

I clean out my cutlery drawer once a fortnight because one day it will look fine and the next I'll be like, 'What the hell is that in there?' It seems to be a haven for crumbs.

I'll take all the cutlery out, whack it in the sink in some Fairy Liquid and warm water, and while they're soaking I'll use my worktop hoover, Shelley Shark, to get all the bits out of the corners. Then I'll disinfect it and put everything back in once it's dry.

MY FAVOURITE
HINCH ROUTINES

Hinch Half-Hour

I do think it's really good to have a goal with cleaning, and my favourite thing is the hinch half-hour.

I'll write a list of what I would ideally like to get done, set a timer on my phone and I'm good to go. I'll tick things off as I go and it definitely motivates me to keep going. There is nothing quite like that feeling when you can cross something off your list.

I'm like a whirlwind and I keep going back to my list and checking it regularly. I'll also make a note if I'm running out of anything so I can stock up when I go shopping and do a hinch haul. As one of my followers put it, going shopping for cleaning products is my equivalent of a kid going toy shopping. It brings me so much happiness.

If I check my timer and I've still got some time left to do more jobs, I'll add a couple of cheeky things to my list just to give myself that extra spring in my step. And if I get to the end of those jobs and still have a few seconds to spare? I'm a happy lady.

The Clockwise Clean

The beauty of the clockwise clean is that you don't miss anything, and you don't feel like it's all too overwhelming. Sometimes when you walk into a room you can look and think, 'There's too much to do in here, I'm never going to finish it,' and walk out. But if you walk into a room with your cleaning basket full of your favourite must-haves, start to your left (that's your 12 o'clock), work your way around the room (1,2, 3 o'clock), and then end up back where you started having circled the room, you know it's all been taken care of.

If I start a room feeling a bit out of sorts I know that by the time I get to the end I'll feel calmer. It's like I'm emptying my mind as I'm completing another task. And I don't care if it's tragic, I get so excited when I'm near the end.

When I get to the ottoman in my living room I know I've only got the lamp and the table to do and my work here is done. It's great to have that finishing point.

I would always recommend taking your daily cleaning basket and your wipes basket into the room of your choice so you know you've got all the bits you need. It's annoying when you have to keep going back and forth to the kitchen because it distracts you.

Fresh'n Up Friday

Personally, my perfect Friday night in would be lighting my candles, getting the wax melts going and choosing the perfect TV line-up. Me, Jamie and Henry sit on the sofa under a huge blanket waiting for our favourite Chinese takeaway to be delivered! On the other hand, my perfect night 'out out' involves all the girls starting off at my house for pre-drinks and hair and make-up prep, and then it's off into town to dance the night away, or, even better, to find a karaoke bar! If only Henry could come! But whether you're having a night in or a night out, there's no better feeling than knowing that your house is freshly hinched on a Friday! Waking up on that Saturday morning – be it fresh as a daisy or absolutely hanging – you'll feel incredible knowing there's one less thing that needs to be done and this always makes me feel more in control of my life.

Doing a Fresh'n Up Friday clean will give you the opportunity to have a lazy Saturday – which, let's be honest, we all need from time to time! This is how I go about it: simply go around every room in the house and write down a maximum of three things in each room you would like to get done. No matter how big or small. It's up to you. Note them all down room by room and, once you've got your list, take it around the house with you and tick it off as you go. Little tip: once you've compiled your list of three things you want to achieve in each room, collate all of the products that you need to get each task done and take them around the house with you in your basket. This saves you from having to go back and forth to your Narnia, which wastes precious Friday-night time!

DIARY

————————————

○ My perfect Friday night in is . . .

....

....

....

....

....

....

....

○ My perfect Friday night 'out out' is . . .

....

....

....

....

....

....

....

DIARY

○ Which room do you enjoy cleaning
most?

....
....
....

○ Which cleaning task is your number-
one favourite?

....
....
....

○ Which one would you happily never
do again?

....
....
....

○ How do you keep your Narnia
organised?

....
....
....

o How do you make your sofa feel cosy?
....
....
....

o What does your favourite warm
   blanket look like?
....
....
....

o What is your number-one kitchen
   gadget?
....
....
....

o What is your signature dish?
....
....
....

PART FIVE
Let's De-Clutter Our Lives!

CHAPTER TEN

HARRY HINCH
AND THE TRUNK
OF JUNK

My understairs cupboard is one of those places that just seems to fill up with 'stuff'. Honestly, I'll open it one day and it looks pretty tidy, and then the next day it's shocking. It's like little elves have been in there and moved stuff around and made it messier. I call it my Harry Potter cupboard and after I cleared it out properly and made it look nice a regular Harry Hinch became essential.

Every now and again I have to do a real blitz and pull

everything out and start again. I'll put things into a giant pile and then separate it out into 'junk' and 'good'. The junk goes to the charity shop or in the bin and the good goes back in. But not before I've cleaned it out fully and given it a good going-over with Sharon the Shark.

When I put everything back last time I added key hooks, a broom holder and some baskets, and even hung up a few pics – it has never looked better.

JUNK TRUNK

I own a junk trunk, aka my ottoman, which used to terrify me every time I looked in it. While it may be beautiful on the outside, inside it was a horror show.

Jamie puts his tools in there sometimes, which upsets me no end because they belong in the garage, but I'm usually responsible for the rest of the things that gather. But now I have it down to a T! I found three baskets that sit inside perfectly and in those baskets live 1) my wax melts collection, 2) stationery and Sellotape, and 3) leads, cables and chargers. I love keeping it organised now.

GARAGE

As you know, I'm all about the storage in my garage, especially the wondrous Narnia. If you ever have any furniture that you decide doesn't go with your décor any more but you don't want to chuck it, pop it in your garage. I had a chest of drawers that I got really good use out of and I didn't want to throw it out, so I popped it in there and Jamie keeps his tools in one drawer and car cleaning equipment in another. It keeps it so organised.

Your garage is an extension of your home so treat it nicely. I've even got pictures up on the wall. It doesn't have to be a cold, unhappy place. Cheer your garage up with some nice things.

I've got bike racks on the wall. They're incredible because bikes take up a massive amount of room, so racks get them up and out of the way.

PESKY PAPERS

Papers are so annoying because they generally end up all over the place and you can never find what you need when you need it. This is another top tip I picked up from my mum when I was growing up – box it all up. It's that simple.

Whenever we used to go through catalogues together

Mum always used to keep any documentation relating to what she bought in a box with a lid so it all stayed together. Even if it was an old shoebox or something, it did the job.

She kept a plastic wallet in the same box and put all our receipts in there. Whenever Dad or one of us kids said, 'Do you know where this letter is?' or 'Do you know where the receipt for so and so is?' she always knew where it was, so it was hassle-free.

Every Saturday she would go through the box with her calculator and pay things off and make sure her filing system was in order. It wasn't exactly complex but it really worked. I used to love sitting there watching her doing her life admin and I always wanted to play along!

I follow the same system now and if post comes I'll read it or I'll leave it on the side for Jamie to read. If it's rubbish I'll shred it and recycle it, and if it's something we need to keep it goes into my box of papers.

It's an A4 box a friend gave me as a present one year and it works a treat. I've added a small plastic wallet I got from the post office for my receipts and now I feel like a secretary myself.

Every six months, Jamie and I will go through that box and shred anything we don't need to keep. I love using the shredder so much, it's the best. It cost me around £20, from eBay of course. I feel really relaxed once that box has been cleared out and the shredder has eaten up all our old bills or confidential info.

RECYCLING

I am all for recycling. People are sometimes negative about the fact that I use products that are in plastic containers. It's not ideal, but I do recycle everything I possibly can and try to do something positive about it.

I'm all for helping any charitable causes as much as I can! You have probably seen my visit to Dogs Trust. It was just amazing! The donations made off the back of my story were unbelievable, so thank you so much for the support, Hinchers! And another particular charity, called Kicks Count, deserves so much recognition. Basically, you bag up your used cleaning products, send them off to a company called TerraCycle and it generates money for the charity. I talked about it on my stories and they gained a lot of sign-ups. So as much as I understand the plastics side is not great, I am really trying to help out where I can. Just imagine if all my Hincher followers recycled their plastics! Imagine the difference that would make! Please don't forget to recycle and follow @kicks.count on Instagram.

CHAPTER ELEVEN

TOP HINCHES

HOW I GOT MY WARDROBE UNDER CONTROL!

There aren't many things that are as upsetting as a messy wardrobe. I looked in mine one day and I thought, 'That's got to be revamped.' My clothes were all on mismatched hangers, some had fallen on the floor, the door was struggling to close, and it certainly didn't look organised.

I found some lovely grey felt hangers on eBay which were so reasonably priced. I find they are the best for keeping clothes in the right place. I replaced all of my old hangers so now they're all the same and it looks much neater.

I clear my wardrobe out at the end of summer and winter

because then I can pack away all the clothes I know I won't wear for another six months or so. They'll go under the bed in storage bags or into the garage until I need them again.

I think the best things to use for storing clothes are vacuum bags. Obviously I go for the scented ones! I take out any clothes I haven't worn for a while, fold them and whack them in. Mate, they are a life-changer.

The first time I used them I was shocked that they actually worked but now I'm obsessed. I would honestly happily pack more clothes away just so I could go through the process of attaching the hoover, sucking all the air out and watching as my clothes shrink to the size of a toddler's. I'm not going to lie; the clothes can be pretty creased when you get them out to wear again, but I think that's a small price to pay for the utter joy of it all.

I wasn't quite so joyful when I asked Jamie to put my vacuum-packed clothes into storage for me last year and he took them to the clothes bank. True story. I had to ask him to go back and get them for me. Lucky for him, they were still there!

TOP TIP: Don't forget to pack away your seasonal shoes or boots. People often forget to put shoes away and they take up so much room in your wardrobe.

I stay on top of my wardrobe by using the same technique as my end-of-year clear-out. If I haven't worn something for a year, it goes. I also look at what kind of condition something is in. Even if you love it, if it looks faded, old or bobbly you're not going to feel good in it.

If I love something I will wear it quite a lot, and I don't believe in chucking something out just because everyone's seen me in it before. I think that's crazy.

I used to feel really guilty about getting rid of clothes or not wearing them enough, but now I don't. Set it free for someone else to enjoy. It's just taking up space. If you feel really bad you can always sell it on eBay or Depop.

Clothes banks are amazing because even if something has got a little hole in it there are people who will mend them and send them off to countries that really need them. So don't be scared of giving away something that's not perfect.

I preserve my clothes by not necessarily washing every item each time I wear it because you don't always need to. Some people overwash their clothes. If you wash them too often they'll potentially lose their colour or go out of shape. If I only wear something for a few hours around the house and then put my pyjamas on, I'm very happy to Febreze it, pop it away and wear it again.

I carry on my bargain hunting into my wardrobe. My favourite vests are from Zara and they're £5.99. Labels make no difference to me, and I don't think you always get what you pay for. Okay, a cashmere jumper can be amazing and it's going to be better quality than a really cheapie one, but other than that, it's so hard to tell how much things cost.

I don't own a single designer handbag or designer pair of shoes. The only designer thing I've ever had is a pink Ralph Lauren jumper that Jamie bought me a couple of years ago. You can have the most beautiful Gucci shoes and Balenciaga bags, but at the end of the day we've all still got to clean our loos, huns.

There's nothing wrong with working hard and saving up to treat yourself to a nice designer purchase, but, to me, jeans are jeans and leggings are leggings. As my followers know, my favourite leggings for winter are thermal Primark ones and they're a total barg. You don't need to spend £20 on a pair of plain black leggings for them to be decent quality.

Everyone went mad for my Linzi shoes and they were £30. Unless someone was to come up to you and demand to know what label your clothes are, they're never going to know. And if you feel comfortable and happy in something, you're going to look amazing no matter how much you paid for it. If I'm perfectly honest, the majority of my wardrobe is made up of comfy lounge sets, purely because this is my favourite thing to hinch in!

I get asked a lot about my make-up routines, so here's a list of my current favourite products. (Please note: this changes quite a lot because I love experimenting!)

MY MAKE-UP MUST-HAVES

No Poreblem Primer by Touch in Sol

*

Estée Lauder Double Wear foundation in
Tawny

*

Laura Mercier Flawless Fusion concealer
(I use this under my eyes)

*

Hourglass Veil Translucent Setting Powder

*

MAC Mineralize Skinfinish in Dark Tan
for contouring

*

BECCA highlighter in Champagne Pop

*

Hourglass Girl Lip Stylo Explorer

*

MAC In Extreme Dimension Lash
Mascara

*

NARS black eyeliner

*

Paige Lash Magnifique eyelashes

*

Hourglass eyebrow sculpting pencil

*

Charlotte Tilbury Lip Liner

*

ICONIC setting spray and highlighters

TOP TIP: My make-up drawer used to be a beauty fail, until a Hincher recommended drawer dividers to me and they changed everything. Now I've sectioned all of my make-up out it looks beautiful. I am easily pleased.

Don't Forget to Clean Your Make-Up Brushes!

Think about it, these go on your face every day. Every day! Who knows what's living in them? They're every bit as important as our Barry bristle brushes.

HINCH YOUR MAKE-UP BRUSHES

○ Wet the bristles with lukewarm water and place a drop of make-up-brush cleanser of your choice (or liquid soap) on to a make-up cleansing mat. I would strongly recommend investing in one of these beauties because they get into all of those annoying nooks and crannies.

- Gently massage and rotate the tips of the bristles on the cleansing mat and enjoy watching the built-up product run free.

- Repeat until the brush runs clear.

- <u>Little Tip:</u> Make sure you keep the brushes face down at all times so the water doesn't run into the metal section or the handle. That's where the glue is and it holds the hairs together.

- Smooth the brushes into shape and allow them to dry.

TOP TIP: I do have a make-up hinch highlight on my Instagram page, so feel free to check that out, Hinchers, if you haven't already!

PACKING HINCH

I will hold my hands up and admit I am not the best packer because I always want to try and pack everything I own, but I have got better. A bit. This is how I do it.

The very first thing I do is write a list of everything I need to pack. Obviously that includes a Minkeh and a small bottle of Zoflora in case the hotel room needs a bit of a going-over.

I make sure my Lenor-infused tumble dryer sheets are ready so I can put them in between everything I pack so my clothes smell good the other end.

I always put clothes in first, folded, not rolled, just because that's how my mum taught me to do it. She does often help me to pack because she has a magic way of fitting everything in.

My toiletries always go into waterproof bags in case anything leaks.

I tick everything off my list as I go along and then I don't have to stress about forgetting anything when I get to the airport.

HANDBAG HINCH

Keeping my handbag clean and tidy is one of the number-one things for me. I hate it when I try to find my phone and I have to wade through a mountain of tissues and hair bands.

Let's face it, whatever we do, rubbish does build up in our handbags. I will go through mine every few days and clear it out, but because I use it every day, by the time I do it, it's built up again.

HINCH YOUR HANDBAG

---

o Whenever I get in from shopping, I'll put all of my receipts in my little plastic wallet so they're out of the way. And as we all know, it's always the one you can't find that you need! If you don't empty out your receipts, your purse ends up bulging at the seams and you'll end up losing them.

o I wipe my purse out with a gentle anti-bac wipe every couple of weeks too, because you would not believe how dirty it gets.

- I always have an empty make-up bag in my handbag too, so if I want to take make-up out with me I can put it in there rather than just chucking it in loose.

- I have another little bag for my medication so that's not free-floating. If you've got some little bags it means if you do put other things in you can then find them easily. It's basically the bag equivalent of your cupboard baskets.

- Once I've taken everything out I'll turn the lining inside out to get rid of any crumbs, and then I'll spritz it with some Febreze.

- I'll rub a gentle anti-bac wipe over the outside of my bag.

- <u>Little Tip</u>: If you get a lipstick or pen mark on your bag, spraying it with hairspray and wiping it with a white cloth works really well on leather, but go easy, and do a patch test first!

CAR HINCH

Mr Hinch loves to keep on top of the car hinching, which is fine by me. He loves cars and enjoys it and that's why you don't see me hinching the car regularly! But if I do ever clean the car, I like to do it in seven simple steps:

HINCH YOUR CAR

○ Use a small car interior bristle brush to pick out all dust and dirt from those annoying little crevices.

○ Using Stardrops Leather Clean and Feed and a dry cloth, spray all leather interior.

○ Using your diluted Zoflora spray and dry cloth, wipe down the dash board, steering wheel, all handles, the works! Who wouldn't want their car to smell of Zoflo, mate?

○ Vacuum all mats and floors using Shelley.

- Spray 1001 Carpet Fresh on the floors.

- Empty the car bin, if you have one. If you don't – check them out on eBay! I love mine. Make sure the organza bags of your in-wash scent boosters are still smelling fresh! If not, replace them.

- Replenish your boot stock. I have a boot organiser, which is made up of a blanket, water bowl for Henry, large bottle of water, ice scraper, windscreen cover, small first-aid kit, reusable shopping bags, torch, plenty of handy towels and a windscreen cloth.

CHAPTER TWELVE

HENRY HINCH

Introducing
HENRY HINCH

As my Hinchers know, Henry is literally my life. I've always wanted a dog of my own. My mum and dad had a dog when I was growing up, a miniature schnauzer called Mason, and he was my mum's everything. She didn't have a son so he became like her little boy. We even used to call him 'the boy' (how imaginative! Ha!).

I also had hamsters and rabbits growing up, but it's just not the same as my Henry. I loved my little rabbits, Barney and Yoshi, but you can't take a rabbit for a walk.

As soon as I left my job and started studying hairdressing in the evenings at college, I knew it was the right time to get a dog. I was so excited and had never felt so happy. My sister has a sausage dog called Heskey and a cocker spaniel called Paddy and it made me broody! Well, fur-baby broody I should say!

I get thousands of messages asking Henry's breed because he's so loved by my Hinchers! So here it is . . . Henry is a cocker spaniel, but you get two different types. You get the working cockers, which are very intelligent and need constant stimulation, or show cockers, which are a bit calmer, soppy and more like fur humans to me.

I knew I wanted a show cocker because this is the same breed as Paddy, and he's just a perfect dog! So one day I looked online to see if anyone nearby was selling or adopting puppies. This is going to sound crazy but I did think how funny it would be to get one that would match my hair (they do say dogs look like their owners), so I really wanted a golden one. I knew they existed, I just had to find one!

A lady popped up who lived a few villages away from my parents' house, and she had a litter of golden show cockers for sale. It was fate!

Jamie and I went to see the puppies the same day and as soon as I saw Henry I just knew. We were sat outside in this lady's garden and all the puppies, two boys and three girls, came running out on to the patio area. Henry was the only one that rolled over the patio step instead of stepping over it like the rest! I remember the breeder rolling her eyes and saying, 'Don't worry about him, he's fine. He's rolled over that step so many times.' I fell in love on the spot.

I've still got a video of that day and he had such a personality. He was the biggest and the chubbiest of all the puppies and he had this little white spot on his forehead, which is a birthmark.

Jamie and I paid a deposit on the spot to reserve him and arranged to pick him up when we got back from visiting Jamie's parents in Majorca. I won't lie, it was the longest week of my life because I knew he would be ready to pick up when we got back home. I should have been enjoying the holiday, but all I could think was, 'I'm finally getting a puppy!' I even took a book about cocker spaniels away with me and read it twice over.

We landed back at Stansted Airport at 3pm on a Sunday afternoon and I said to Jamie, 'I don't think I can wait another two days to go and collect him.'

I had his bed, collar, food, toys and everything else ready back at home, and there was just no way I could hang on that long. I knew he was ready to come away from his fur mum so there was nothing stopping us collecting him early if the breeder agreed. And she did!

Bringing Henry home was so amazing. He settled in straight away and was such a joy to be around. But he wasn't always well behaved, as you would expect.

He loved chewing anything and everything, but mainly things that made a noise. He would run and get the post as soon as he heard the letter box go. Then he'd grab the letters and run to my bedroom with them. I discovered him in there one time, lying on the rug and chewing all the letters that had arrived that day.

I knew I had to find a way to keep him occupied and I remembered a good trick my mum used. When kids go round to my parents' house, my mum always gets out a play mat for them, and puts toys out for them.

One day I bought Henry a play mat (yes, an actual baby play mat!) and put his toys on it, and bless him, he stayed on that mat for hours chewing his chews and playing with his toys. After that, whenever the post came he would run and get it but bring it back to the mat. It was like his safe mat, his own space, and if we were to get another dog I would do the same again! It worked so well! I was able to keep a close eye on him at all times.

He didn't bark a lot, and he still doesn't now, unless the window cleaner suddenly appears at the patio doors and then he lets him know he's in the building.

He was such a funny puppy. We spent all our time together because he was the only company I had from six in the morning until six in the evening, when Jamie was at work. I even missed him if I had to pop out to the shops or went to college three evenings a week for two and a half hours. Even though I knew he was okay at home with Jamie, I just wanted to get home to him. I'd put off going to the shops for as long as possible, and even now I don't leave him for more than two to three hours at a time.

If I get him out a little chicken treat stick he knows I'm going out for a little while so he'll make himself comfortable and wait for me. That's his routine – I think routine is key for all dogs. I did think about getting a dog cam for a while, but I worry I would just sit in Morrisons car park watching him walking around, so I may as well stay at home with him!

I used to be a bit scared knowing I would be on my own for hours while I was studying and Jamie was at work, especially when we were still living in the flat. But when I got Henry I stopped being as scared. I found myself talking to him all the time, and just little things like making Henry's breakfast and walking him through the park gave me a really positive focus.

I remember Jamie calling me one afternoon and I suddenly realised that we hadn't spoken all day, and we used to speak every single morning. He said to me, 'I was going to phone but I knew you would call if you needed me, and I just wanted to show you that you're okay. I don't want you to think that I was ignoring you but I also wanted you to realise how far you've come.' It was a lovely moment.

Jamie literally idolises Henry, and I think he loves him even more because he knows what Henry's done for me. There are days when I've felt so unwell or I'm worrying, but because Henry has been there with me it's made it all so much better. He loves a cuddle and he's the soppiest dog going.

I do treat him like my baby, and I know some people find that odd, but that's how it is with us. Some people love the fact that he's got his own bedroom, and some people find it ridiculous.

The whole bedroom business came about because we realised when Henry was very young that he loved pillows. He would jump on the sofa and move all my cushions about that I'd lovingly karate chopped. As soon as he got one into the right position, he'd curl up and put his head on it.

I started to take the cushion off the sofa and put it on the floor so he could lie there, and then one day I thought, 'Why am I doing this? He's got a lovely dog bed there, but he would rather sleep on a hard floor and have a pillow for his head. He needs his own real bed.'

When we moved into our house there was a spare room, and instead of me taking the pillow off the bed and putting it on the floor, I let Henry get on the bed. He jumped up so happily, lay down and whacked his head on the pillow, and that was it. He had the best night's sleep ever.

He used to wake me up quite early every morning, and that day he didn't wake up until 9.30am. That was the latest he'd ever slept in and when he finally stumbled downstairs his face was all crumpled, his hair was all over the place and he looked like the happiest dog you've ever seen.

The following night I tried putting the pillow on the floor and he looked at me as if to say, 'Are you kidding, Mum? I want to get on the bed.' Now, whenever I say, 'Go and get in your bed,' he runs straight up on to his bed and cosies up. He's like the canine version of me.

Henry has made me so much more relaxed about things. I don't know if other cocker spaniels do it, but he quite often spits his food out, then he'll go back and eat it later on. It's all over the floor and I step on it all the time. It's so painful, it's like stepping on Lego.

He'll often go for a midnight feast so when I go down in the morning there will be bits of food all over the kitchen and it doesn't bother me one bit. It must be a bit like when you've got kids and their toys are everywhere. You don't care how messy it is because you love them so much.

People are obsessed with Henry. People message me saying, 'I can't go to bed yet because I haven't seen Henry go to sleep.' I'm having to put him to bed so other people can go to bed! People ask me what he's doing every day and when we're going for our walk, and I really do feel like a proud mum.

I also get asked what I keep in Henry's drawer so I popped it on my story a while ago. It's mainly treats, dog clothes, his lead and collars, his insurance documents, and the Mother's Day cards Jamie gets me from Henry every year. People might think that's crazy but to me he's the most special dog in the world.

I love everything about him. I love his snoring, I love the fact he likes his paws being massaged and will change paws when he wants the other one done. I love how cuddly he is, how he greets me when I come home, how he'll always nick the warm spot you've been sitting in if you get up from the sofa, and how obsessed he is with ham.

I even like the way he drags his bum along the floor when we go to the dog groomers because he hates it so much. I have to pick him up and hand him over to the groomer. He hates being groomed because he hates water and baths and being wet in general. He's not even keen on rain.

I put off taking him as much as possible, but I think he secretly loves how handsome he looks when he's had his fur clipped and his claws cut. He walks out of there like he's sauntering down a catwalk.

He is a pretty good model, to be fair. One of my most popular Instagram posts of Henry was the one of him in the little Easter bonnet. My niece Abi made the bonnet for Easter, but I only made Henry wear it for the picture and then took it off. I'm not that cruel! He's very good at posing for pictures because he knows he always gets half a slice of ham afterwards.

Walking Henry makes me feel calmer than anything. I love it, he loves it and it's an amazing escape. Being around nature and having time to yourself is the best thing. If Henry stops to sniff something it means I have to stand there and wait, so I start looking around and I notice things like peculiar trees or odd-looking flowers. It sounds so silly but it makes you appreciate all the little things that bit more.

These days we're always rushing around checking social media, or we're on our phones messaging, so sometimes we don't see what's around us. I came across a comment once on a picture of Henry which said that they don't see me walking Henry very often on my stories so they're worried I don't do it enough. But the reason is that I don't take my phone with me when I walk him. If I took my phone and documented all of our walks, I wouldn't be able to enjoy them like I do. It's my downtime.

Every now and again I'll do a little boomerang video of him but I like that time to be for us. It's really healthy for my mind.

Of all the things that people have said to me, one person suggesting that I don't walk Henry enough has been the most upsetting. I take him out every single day, at least twice a day, and believe me, if I didn't he wouldn't sleep as much as he does.

Anyone can call my house dull or say it's too grey or mock me for naming my cloths, but when someone said that my dog has the worst life and he was just there to dress up and earn me money, it absolutely broke my heart.

Someone even claimed I didn't walk him because I'm too house proud and don't want muddy paws in my house. I cried over that for hours because it couldn't be further from the truth. I would never usually respond to comments like that but I actually inboxed that person and explained why the walks aren't on my stories. Maybe I shouldn't have done, but it bothered me so much I had to.

My followers often say to me, 'Mrs Hinch, how do you deal with muddy paws or dog hair? He's sleeping on a bed, that might make it dirty.' This is what I tell them about how I hinch Henry!

HINCH YOUR FUR BABIES

_____

○ He's got his own Tessa tea towel, which lives in his basket under the stairs along with his coat, poo bags and lead. So if he comes into the house after we've been for a walk I'll wipe his little paws with it.

○ If Henry comes in and he's got muddy paws I'm really laid-back about it. I've got laminate flooring so I'll whack Vera out and the paw prints are gone in seconds. Henry knows when he comes in that he mustn't go on the rug in the living room so he'll walk around it. It's like he's learnt that if he does he'll make it dirty. He's learnt to hinch and I'm so proud. Ha!

○ I've got a great grooming glove that brushes him as you stroke him so he loves it. It takes all the loose hair off, so it's like a mini groom.

○ He's got dog dry shampoo for when he doesn't need a full-on bath, but he needs a little refresh. I picked it up from Pets At Home and I think it's fab for quickness.

○ Make sure you wash your dog's collars. I'm sure people don't think about it that much. If they're leather, you can wipe them over with leather cleaner, and fabric ones can go in the washing machine. Henry has a few different collars so I can rotate them and clean whichever ones I'm not using. And bicarbonate of soda cleans, refreshes and eliminates odours – it's perfect, so here's a tip:

TOP TIP:
- Fill a bowl half full with hot water
- Add two teaspoons of bicarbonate of soda
- Stir until the soda has dissolved
- Pop the collar in the mix for ten minutes
- Remove, scrub and rinse the collar thoroughly
- Allow to dry completely before popping the collar back on your fur baby
- Done!

○ If your dog runs up the stairs and gets mud on the carpet, whatever you do don't try and wipe it off when it's wet. You may be staring at it wanting to cry but you will be so much better off waiting. Once it's dry I use a Barry bristle brush to brush away the nasties. I hoover up the dried mud, and then use Dr Beckmann carpet stain remover to get rid of leftover marks, if any.

○ I also keep my carpets fur-free using the Squeegee/window scraper method. Whilst this is great for getting hair and fluff out of your carpets, it also has a knack for grabbing tiny dog or cat hairs you wouldn't even know are there.

○ Every night I put a throw over the bed Henry sleeps on, and that can be washed and dried in no time. You can get some really stunning dog beds and they'll look lovely in your home, but some of them are so hard and uncomfortable. I know if I got him one it would just sit there and not get used. A cheap, washable throw on Henry's human bed is what works best for me.

○ I also turn the cushions the other way up so if Henry does happen to get any marks on

them you can't see them. And
if he does, I'll just pop the
pillowcases in the wash and
tumble dry them straight away.

o Every morning I make Henry's bed
and give it a spray with the Dettol
spray because it's great for pets'
beds generally. It keeps his bed fresh
in between changing the sheets and
kills off bacteria. Win-win.

o If anyone comes to stay and
sleeps in Henry's room I always
change the bed sheets, whether
Henry has been lying on them or
not. There is nothing better than
staying in a clean bed with lovely
fresh sheets. You can't beat that
feeling. Because my friends and
family live so close, I rarely have
anyone to sleep over, so yes, it's
Henry's bed and always will be.

o If there's dog hair on the sofa
I use a lint roller that I picked up

from the pound shop. For a quick Henry hinch I brush down the sofa and cushions and then give them a whizz with the Dettol spray or Febreze. That is a five-minute job.

o I'll also use Shelley the handheld Shark to suck up any pet hair or debris. I use her every day anyway so it is no problem at all. Even if Henry rolled in mud and then rolled all over my carpets I would let him off, and I can't say that about any humans.

DIARY

○ How good are you at de-cluttering?

....

....

....

○ What's top of your de-cluttering
  to do list?

....

....

....

○ On a scale of 1–10, how badly do
  you need to do a good wardrobe
  clear-out?

....

....

....

○ How good are your packing skills?

....

....

....

○ What clothes do you like to hinch in?

....
....
....

○ What are your favourite beauty products?

....
....
....

○ What do you do for your downtime?

....
....
....

○ Do you have any pet-hinching tips?

....
....
....

○ What's the best cleaning tip you've learnt in this book?

....
....
....

ALL THE BEST
FOR NOW!

Well, that brings us to the end of the book, Hinchers! I really hope you've enjoyed reading it as much as I've enjoyed working on it. I've absolutely loved getting all my hints and tips down, and also sharing the more personal side of my life with you all. I know from reading your messages that a lot of what I've said will resonate with you. Please remember we are all in this together.

Being able to talk about things so openly makes me realise how far I've come during this (cliché alert!) journey. I've spoken about things I could never have imagined myself being brave enough to disclose a couple of years ago, and I was able to because of the unbelievable support I get from all of you. I really do feel like my Hinchers are my extended family. I know you've always got my back, and I've always got yours.

If I can carry on making others smile, helping people to open up about their anxiety or other mental health issues, and finding new ways to make sinks look shiny and beautiful, I will be the happiest girl in the world. As I've told you before, I'm taking you all on this journey with me, because without you this journey wouldn't exist.

Here's to many more fun times ahead!

Love Soph (aka Mrs Hinch) xx

READY, SET, HINCH!

Okay, Hinchers... To help get you
started I've created the following
checklists for you to fill in...

Happy hinching!

Love Soph xx

HINCH HALF-HOUR

Hinched

- ○ .... ☐
- ○ .... ☐
- ○ .... ☐
- ○ .... ☐
- ○ .... ☐
- ○ .... ☐
- ○ .... ☐
- ○ .... ☐
- ○ .... ☐
- ○ .... ☐
- ○ .... ☐
- ○ .... ☐
- ○ .... ☐
- ○ .... ☐

Hinched

- ☐ ....
- ☐ ....
- ☐ ....
- ☐ ....
- ☐ ....
- ☐ ....
- ☐ ....
- ☐ ....
- ☐ ....
- ☐ ....
- ☐ ....
- ☐ ....
- ☐ ....
- ☐ ....

CLOCKWISE CLEAN

Hinched

- ○ .... ☐
- ○ .... ☐
- ○ .... ☐
- ○ .... ☐
- ○ .... ☐
- ○ .... ☐
- ○ .... ☐
- ○ .... ☐
- ○ .... ☐
- ○ .... ☐
- ○ .... ☐
- ○ .... ☐
- ○ .... ☐
- ○ .... ☐

Hinched

- ○ .... ☐
- ○ .... ☐
- ○ .... ☐
- ○ .... ☐
- ○ .... ☐
- ○ .... ☐
- ○ .... ☐
- ○ .... ☐
- ○ .... ☐
- ○ .... ☐
- ○ .... ☐
- ○ .... ☐
- ○ .... ☐
- ○ .... ☐

FRESH'N UP FRIDAY

Hinched

- ○ .... ☐
- ○ .... ☐
- ○ .... ☐
- ○ .... ☐
- ○ .... ☐
- ○ .... ☐
- ○ .... ☐
- ○ .... ☐
- ○ .... ☐
- ○ .... ☐
- ○ .... ☐
- ○ .... ☐
- ○ .... ☐
- ○ .... ☐

Hinched

- ○ .... ☐
- ○ .... ☐
- ○ .... ☐
- ○ .... ☐
- ○ .... ☐
- ○ .... ☐
- ○ .... ☐
- ○ .... ☐
- ○ .... ☐
- ○ .... ☐
- ○ .... ☐
- ○ .... ☐
- ○ .... ☐
- ○ .... ☐

BACKWARDS HINCH LIST

Hinched

- ○ .... ☐
- ○ .... ☐
- ○ .... ☐
- ○ .... ☐
- ○ .... ☐
- ○ .... ☐
- ○ .... ☐
- ○ .... ☐
- ○ .... ☐
- ○ .... ☐
- ○ .... ☐
- ○ .... ☐
- ○ .... ☐
- ○ .... ☐

Hinched

- ○ .... ☐
- ○ .... ☐
- ○ .... ☐
- ○ .... ☐
- ○ .... ☐
- ○ .... ☐
- ○ .... ☐
- ○ .... ☐
- ○ .... ☐
- ○ .... ☐
- ○ .... ☐
- ○ .... ☐
- ○ .... ☐
- ○ .... ☐

NOTES

NOTES

NOTES

NOTES

....

....

....

....

....

....

....

....

....

....

....

....

....

....

NOTES

....

....

....

....

....

....

....

....

....

....

....

....

....

....

NOTES

NOTES

Fur baby sleeping...